Dog Heart

ALSO BY BREYTEN BREYTENBACH

A Season in Paradise

The True Confessions of an Albino Terrorist

Return to Paradise

The Memory of Birds in Times of Revolution

Dog Heart

A MEMOIR

———

Breyten Breytenbach

HARCOURT BRACE & COMPANY
New York   San Diego   London

Library of Congress Cataloging-in-Publication Data
Breytenbach, Breyten.
Dog heart: a memoir/Breyten Breytenbach.—1st ed.
p.   cm.
ISBN 0-15-100458-7
1. Breytenbach, Breyten.
2. Authors, Afrikaans—20th century—
Biography.   I. Title.
PT6592.12.R4Z465   1999
839.3'615—dc21   98-47017

Text set in Bell MT
Designed by Lori McThomas Buley
Printed in the United States of America
First edition
A C E D B

To the memory of
Rachel Susanna Keet

Et ce livre que j'écris, remonte dans mon souvenir d'instants délicieux, est, mais le dirais-je? l'accumulation de ces instants afin de dissimuler ce grand prodige: "Il n'y avait rien à voir, ni à entendre..."

JEAN GENET
Un Captif Amoureux

The man who finds his country sweet is only a raw beginner; the man for whom each country is as his own is already strong; but only the man for whom the whole world is a foreign country is perfect.

ERICH AUERBACH
as quoted by Edward Said

Dog Heart

BEGINNING, FOR THE READER

To cut a long story short: I am dead.

Do you think I'm joking? Am I not lurking behind these rustling words—perhaps a little thicker around the waist, a little darker in the mind? Am I not the writer sitting in the dappled light of the pepper tree, pursing my lips and closing my eyes to the glare of a yellow fire baking the valley?

Mind fumbles for a buried reference; I'm on the verge of remembering the odour of ancient clods. Can one touch the moon?

Yes and no. Obviously I'm writing. Look, I'm even leaning forward to whisper to you. Don't worry. There's nothing I want. I won't bother you, and I won't fall down. The ways of the mirror are dark to the eye.

But no, when I look into the mirror I know that the child born here is dead. It has been devoured by the dog. The dog looks back at me and he smiles. His teeth are wet with blood. This has always been a violent country. Writing is an after-death activity, a sigh of remorse.

I return to this land now that time has gone away. I try to identify the shadows and talk to the baboons who walk on all fours to avoid being taken for people; the dog growls and I climb the tree, like my grandfather, to watch out for floods and for snakes. Look high, look low!

BONNIEVALE

It is early summer when we drive over to Bonnievale for the annual cheese and wine festival. Bright sheets of sunlight on the hills, flowers along the road bunching their colours, the jacaranda trees stained a pale purple. Then fields of shade like bruised mouths when loose-fitting clouds race before the sun and light's throat suddenly grows deep.

On our way the four of us—Adam and his red-haired lady friend Mercy (who doesn't know that she is coloured), my wife Lotus and I—visit the Van Loveren wine farm, upriver, towards Ashton, to taste their cabernet sauvignon. We tongue the elixir around our mouths, then load several boxes in the boot of the car. One of the Retief brothers, estate owners, comes and goes with cap tilted over a crooked smile and trousers hanging on for dear life and decency just below the bulging belly, to keep pouring from a full bottle.

A fragrant garden shades the back of the wine cellars. Jeanne Retief, the materfamilias, says: Yes, but who tamed the land? Who dug the irrigation channel and brought vines to this soil? Now the government paints us as intruders, but did they who were here before us ever plant a single tree? She knows. For fifty years or more she has been looking after every bush and shrub greening this unexpected paradise. She marked each major event by planting a sapling and bestowing upon it an appropriate name. Her eyes are two ancient tortoises hiding under the weathered stone of her face. *Verwoerd*, there (she points), soughing with birds; the fir is called *Republic*, it grew fast; *King George* needs a lot of water, a thirsty bugger; *D. F. Malan* was a shaggy palm tree, but he got blown over in the big wind; a rather rakish young *Mandela*, he will still grow in stature, of that you may be sure. The clouds need company.

In the main street we stop before cousin Aletta's shop where lady's drawers and buttons and spools of thread and millinery and daintily printed bales of cloth can be seen through the glass front. The road surface has not been upgraded in fifty years. This is the town where I was born, those were the humpbacked hills riding the skyline in sombre procession, like old songs, and further back the same mountain range is still blocking off the interior. The badlands beyond the escarped blue horizon is known as *Moordenaarskaroo*, a dry inner heart where murderers and robbers and escaped slaves and runaway soldiers could find refuge. To be devoured by sun. The Breërivier: wide and soft and afloat with silvery clouds. The road which snakes along the green banks to slither through the agglomeration is called *Boesmanspad*. White settlers pen off a first farm near the river crossing— *Boesmansdrift*. Later comes the project to build a village. Khoisan country; at least, these valleys and passes and crossings are used by them as they follow migrating animals to fresh pastures. I come and I go here, but once it slips away from my eyesight I can never again locate the birth-house: it becomes confused with someone else's memory.

Red soil in the sorrowful shade of a hill, pencilled in

by the sharper ultramarine shadows of cemetery cypresses and blue gums cupping the skeletons of my paternal grandparents, Oupa Jan and Ouma Annie. Worms and ants have digressed upon their story.

We have to ring a bell for Aletta to come and open the barred door. She is bereft of speech when she sees us. Her husband, Gielie, appears from a back room, wipes his mouth on a broad wrist and says: Well, I'll be damned! Knock me over with a goose feather!

No, we won't stay for lunch, thank you very much. We just came to shake hands.

Marquee tents and stalls are pitched around the rugby grounds near the school. Drum majorettes march back and forth on the grass field. They are small, but already wise to the art of sashaying with high knees and wobbly hips thrown to the wind of eyes. Must be their first important outing, all dollied up in silk. My schooling also started here; I still hear the rumour of excitement. Of course, it was all-white then; the shaded half of the population kept out of sight, or were present differently, at the back door. By the looks of it brown and white now move together effortlessly. Wine certainly helps. The school is integrated, the majorettes coloured.

After the high-stepping dolls will come a show of skills by police with their dogs. One cop plays the role of pickpocket, exaggerating a hooligan sway and swagger, cap pulled down over the ears (it's Saturday, see, the loudspeaker voice explains, which in this rural environment adds up to 'weekly shopping' and 'drunkenness'); he filches a purse from somebody's pocket; a dog is slipped from its leash, runs the villain down, its wet teeth chattering at him. The thief, though white, is supposed to be brown, the dog handler white, one feigns not to notice. Polite applause.

Still later the law enforcers will be followed by teams of bulky men plowing furrows with dug-in heels in a tug-of-war, and lithe youngsters will run sack races. True country sports much favoured by the local farming community. Except that the participants now are mostly brown people.

This is the way it ought to be, like this it looks right, Adam remarks as our eyes feast on the crowd. Yeah, and so self-evident, I agree. Have you noticed how the people look alike? They walk the same way, they speak with the same turn of tongue. Must be because they are fashioned by a shared region and climate. Sure, he confirms, they have similar problems. Maybe they all dream only one story at night. Don't you also think people are actually shaped by natural conditions?

If only it could remain like this! If only 'foreigners' wouldn't come to dislocate local relations!

People are shortish in stature, stout but not fat, and of like swarthy countenance. They seem to share a disregard for the shape of waists. The calves of their legs are well-defined and they plant their feet firmly on the ground. Men generally have a weakness for shorts; many women wear headcloths (*kopdoeke*). Their gestures, their sitting-and-standing, are movements of one pattern.

In front of his booth a trader half-identifies me. Exclaims: Just remind me now, who are you again? He tells of how he used to lodge in the backyard of my uncle, the one with the prominent Adam's apple and the laugh of a rusty wheelbarrow pushed uphill, who used to swing from the curtains at night and who lost his teeth and all his money as well on the horses because he just barely missed reading correctly his premonitory dreams, and who was so very emaciated when he died, sometimes one needs a coffin in order not to be blown away. I can only answer obliquely. He asks who Adam might be. I reply that he's my brother. We do look quite a lot alike.

In the drinks tent we proceed from one table to the next. Food can also be had—*bobotie* (curried mince) and *waterblommetjiebredie* (a stew of water lilies). Weltevreden's proprietor fills our glasses with the crystal-clear, pale yellow sap of his most recent blends; on his estate they still produce a limited number of bottles from an old vineyard, purely for sentimental reasons, they call it 'Oupa se wyn' (Grandfather's wine). The Jonkers (my father already claimed) are the lords of the district. Maybe he thought so because he, and his father before him, farmed on land rented from the owners of that big white homestead. A girl Breytenbach married into their ancestry, and Lourens Jonker will now all of a sudden remember that he and his kind are furthermore distantly related to the Cloetes, my mother's family, so we must actually be cousins! A blue eye twinkles, the moustache is standing neatly assembled to attention below the barely veined nose of the connoisseur. It is his considered opinion that we were in the habit of making music together when we were very young. After all, are we not models of the same year? At the house of Aunt Such-and-Such. Remember? He the piano and I the guitar? Afterwards I will realize he must be confusing me with my brother.

A brown gentleman with dark glasses comes up to pump my hand enthusiastically. Principal of the school in Happy Valley just outside town. On the other side of the hill. And when are you coming to visit the coloured community? (This is a reproach.) Several of his staff are with him. A missis wants to know why our visit had not been announced, isn't it a shame, surely it is practically as momentous as the coming of our president? No, but we are here to enjoy the normal life. The sun and the sighing of shadows. When wind moves through a copse of trees, it makes the sound of a very slow sea. As the principal switches to Afrikaans he takes off the dark glasses; with English he will put them back on again. He is still angry and unhappy, even if at present he doesn't quite know why—but wasn't everything supposed to be different? A man with a yellow smile pinches the amenable bum of the chubby schoolmistress... A burly white man comes to chuck his voice into the hubbub, he must be my elder by about ten years. Says my father drove the bus in which he rode to school every morning all these many years ago. 'Oom Hannes', he remembers the name. Says we used to live in a little reed-thatched structure out yonder against the hillside. He looks with some annoyance into the dark recesses of the school principal's spectacles: Take off that bloody thing, man. This guy speaks Afrikaans just like you and I do.

Outside the tent we move around the corner to drink coffee in the shade of a pepper tree. In this country one is served large cups of stained cat-lap called 'coffee'. A disputable definition... One of the teachers brings a younger man to our table. He too is confused by the languages and the forms of address. He addresses me as *meneer*, but when he speaks to the woman he refers to me as the 'comrade'. He is the vice-chair of the local ANC branch. They are having some internal disagreements, which is why locally the movement couldn't win the last elections. It would seem—certainly because he doesn't know where exactly to situate me—that he expects me to arbitrate these differences. But this cannot be, my voice is long since as mute as that of a Muscovy duck when it comes to liberation politics, and perhaps he is confusing me with my brother. (The Muscovy duck is from the East.)

MEMORY

Why, after all these years, do I feel the urge to go and look for the other one, the child I must have been? To walk the dead? To lay a shadow to rest? Had I died then, the corpse would have been buried among the whites, a rotten heart, the hump of soil neatly heaped with periwinkle shells which in time would have been whittled to broken teeth of silver foil, or moonflakes. A long time ago I used to be scared by bigger kids telling the story of an earthworm living in the cemetery, as white and as grown as a hairless child. At night, so the story went, the worm would emerge from some grave and wail piteously. To die then would have meant going to meet the worm. No wonder we didn't want to go anywhere near the spot.

There should be a trace at least. Oh, nothing much—an infant corpse would have needed no more space than a small dead dog left in a manger. Perhaps a faded headstone or an angel with the features eaten away by rain? Under what name, though? Aunt Tina, Oupa Jan's darling daughter, insisted that I be called Breyten to preserve something of her maiden name, the paternal ancestry. I would be her 'adopted' child since she didn't have any of her own. Her husband, Uncle Willy Campbell, so much wanted to be a father. Perhaps I'm hoping now to find a narrow hand of soil and a sign saying *B. Breytenbach*, or *B. Campbell*—a thought forgotten before it was ever properly uttered.

And nothing. Not a whisper. Sun glinting on sea-shells. Sure, there is a bone orchard of Breytenbachs—Oupa Jan and Ouma Annie in their moss-covered time-ship, other members of the extended clan too, unfamiliar names with rotted-away faces, for it is known that bad blood between the various branches rubbed away the memories, and then those who entered by marriage, a Keet here and a Wentzel or Olivier there. Only, no memory of myself.

A cloud throws cool tracks over the earth. But I am dead, don't you see? And now the worm has destroyed even the imprint in the ground. No hollow for my foot to fit in. How can one live next to one's own absence?

Have I come here to read the prints in the dust, to speak about the light of youth, and how my memories got mixed up with those of others? You will hear many stories. Do be careful with memory.

Because we find many ways of devouring ourselves. The writer, the word eater, is a visitor to all the associations. A night thief, proceeding by allusion and reference, he strips the trees of their meanings and their images. Writing is a painting into which you may walk with a book in your hand. The Original Mind, which harbours no destination, allows for a lot of walking.

To write is to make memory visible, and this memory uncovers a new landscape. When the tree of writing is shaken all manner of things come crashing down—fruit, empty tin cans with exotic labels, birds still calling their names, birds' nests, books, bicycles, even dead resistance fighters or a lamed angel who was hiding among the leaves from the wings of darkness. When I say 'dead people', as in the previous sentence, the shadow of the patriarch is evoked. Or a Khoisan herder.

The dreams of the dead cannot die. There is no expiration date for their souvenirs since they didn't live to see a solution to their anguish. They continue walking in us, we hear their steps like a heartbeat. They are obliged to keep remembering us and also those who come after us.

My daughter Gogga asks whether I believe in reincarnation: shouldn't you, as a Buddhist? And since she knows all the answers already she gives her own version. Conscious life the way we know it is like a glass of water, she says. When it is dropped the glass is broken and you can no longer use it. But the water never disappears. It may evaporate and one day rain will come down on us.

Heaven is a floating cloud reminding the landscape of cooling passages. Our bodies are made of glass. The proof is that when one opens the earth one may cut a finger. When I look at her I see my father's eyes. He also has this habit of resting his eyes upon my face.

Distance is chronology and memory is imagination. It is a given, constant area, a breathing space, a veritable heartland: a lung of time singing our movement towards death, and maybe even making it possible. Just as you cannot survive without dreams, you cannot move on without the memory of where you come from, even if that journey is fictitious. Is what we call identity not that situation made up of the bits and pieces which we remember from previous encounters, events and situations, memory hanging from the branches?

With time some images will fade away, only because the territory of memory, like a ship's wake or a bird's cage, is circumscribed. There cannot be room for everything. The catchment area, the observation field, become saturated. The tree groans under its weight. One may say the road finishes when one can no longer see the peaks and the twists, when the land of sleep becomes barren and bread is changed to stone. Now I am dead, and distance and space will be dust. Memory will be emptied like a glass held to lifeless lips.

And imagination? It must be the discovery of new possibilities to dress up memory, like going back over my tracks to explore another direction, an option of re-situating myself before that which happened in the meantime screwed up my choices. Death is the birth of imagination.

Does the child arrive in life with a knowledge of the past? A ragbag of parents' memories, parts of which will be so patterned as to shape a motif? Does the child have flags in the head? Is it looking for wind? It would seem that the infant's memory is limpid, the space unpolluted. Just below the amniotic fluid behind my face in the mirror the submerged mountains are still visible. Atlantis is a reality.

This must be forgotten for the child I am to become the man I am now. The human is an angel who unlearns the remembrance of nothingness. I must first learn to forget so that I may start to remember others. This passage to entwinement with the souvenirs of others, this bastardisation of zones of experience, doesn't make for a bigger space, it just makes it different.

Maybe memory is the wind among leaves. Maybe memory is an illusion. Maybe it is an illusion which we invent to protect ourselves against the light of time which cannot be stopped, which eats our faces, and against the sorrow of not being able to bring back moments and orgasms. So we invent history to give us substance and presence. We find a thread of continuity

to hang on to over the abyss of absence and nonexist-
ence. Walking becomes a way in itself.

MY GRANDFATHER

My grandfather spends his later days in an ancient pepper tree planted long before my time, and his, not far
from the humble abode in which he and my grandmother live out their twilight years. Ouma Annie is his
second spouse, the mother of my father and his two
siblings. Grandpa's first wife, Aunt Tina's mother, died
after being bitten by a snake in the woodpile. Everybody
in the family pretends that it is perfectly normal to
perch on a branch some ten feet above the ground. He
is not the only one either; in the district several more
old men squat among the leaves, perhaps with an ancient memory of the disastrous flood, or further back,
the war against the imperialist British. *Boom-Boere* (tree
Afrikaners) they are called. It is my task to bring him
his early-morning mug of coffee. He will already be
staring in the direction of the cemetery in the dark em-
brace of a nearby hill untouched by sunlight. Only once,
when I ask him what he is waiting for, does he mutter:
That snake is coming back. As he grows more frail my
father has the tree chopped down out of concern for
Grandpa's safety. We don't want him to break a leg, or
worse. My grandfather never leaves his bed after that
and within a week he is dead.

WELLINGTON

Wellington's Huguenot High School, where I matricu-
lated years ago, asks by mouth of its headmaster

whether my wife, Lotus, and I would consent to being received ceremoniously by the old students' union. I have no objection, just as long as 'people with gold chains around their necks' don't try to profit politically from the event, and provided it doesn't become a circus. Appointment is made for a Saturday night. On Monday morning I will address the senior pupils.

We are given the use of a car. We will lodge in a charming cottage on the guest farm Diemersfontein, fully equipped and including a provision of dried fruit in the pantry. Oak-tree branches scrape over the roof and clouds scrape over the moon's face. The stately farmhouse, a luxury liner beached among the vines, is still partly hidden behind a plantation of eucalyptus trees. In its own lost time it must have lorded over surroundings of well-ordered fields and unpopulated skylines. Now it finds itself hemmed in by a sea of new residential projects. The past must be rebuilt. But also squatter camps and informal settlements rowing ever closer over the rise and through the bushes.

(Just about all of the seven or eight kilometers distancing Wellington from Paarl is now a built-up area. When I was young I whooshed on a bicycle from the one town to the other. There was open veld on both sides of the road; in fact, in my mind I see people with their mouths closed by beards hunting leopard and wild buck in the thickets. Already smoke on the horizon signals two concentrations of illegal migrant labourers and their dependants. Are they the remnants of nomads moving from one sanctuary to the next along the fringes of a 'tamed' colony? *Sakkieskamp* and *Blikkiesdorp* ('Jute-camp' and 'Tin-town'). Those are dangerous places, one knows, probably people sacrifice goats there to appease the spirits of the fathers, and I think I can hear drums beating. Sun flashes off the hovels cobbled together from waste material: glittering settlements of crystal and diamonds.)

(And halfway between Wellington and Paarl there's a cluster of dilapidated houses inhabited by people of colour. Morning glory, the poor man's blueness of flower, trails its little trumpets of purple wind through the weeds of neglected gardens where lean mongrels throttled by ropes tied to posts howl a froth of fury and fear. The odd café with faded Coca-Cola and Joko Tea signboards has its *stoep* heavily protected by chicken wire. Newtown, it is called. From here periodically passing motorists would be stoned. I remember flexed arms holding rocks and distorted mouths hurling curses, but I don't hear a sound. Memory is a silent movie. Maybe one was told all this. My bike's handlebar is decorated with a green ribbon and I'm a world champion leaning into the rush of movement singing around my ears.)

Freek the whale watcher and his girlfriend, Iza, come from Kleinbos by the sea to share the hospitality of a weekend with us. My brother Kwaaiman and his wife and my sister Rachel will join us for the reception.

Nothing much has changed in town, and yet it is but a décor, an empty stage where youthful clamour and the inchoate but hot longings which come later still linger as after-sounds. White is the tall steepled church, white the houses where the white people live. Of the parents' home only the empty shell still holds, with neither crab nor snail to substantiate life. Henceforth the building is to be used as a day clinic for the poor of the earth who are racked by hardy coughs or who suffer from night sweats.

The reception takes place at 'La Provence'—originally the name of a farm attributed to a landsick Huguenot (and we know now that these refugees were scruffy and impoverished 'little people' just about deported from Holland, not the noble pioneers subsequent whitewashers made them out to be), but it is a long time ago already that the meadows and the dams and the vineyards and the dreams were absorbed within the town's delimitations.

We meet the school principal and his wife—good and unpretentious people. She has a head of white hair, he has a face like a rose in bloom. Also a number of teachers and some retired masters. One or two from my time, instinctively I'll 'sir' them as in earlier years. Then, here and there, a classmate. Or not?

One shouldn't give in to these moments. They upset too much. One stares with unseeing eyes and a foolish smile down the years, one sees smoke tendrils and cascading fog and estrangement and the small twists and turns of change in which one did not participate. This bald man, could it be . . . ? And that scrawny woman, surely . . . ? These are my people and I do not know them. My memory has shrunk to the imagined borders of its own making. I recognize the sweet nostalgia of gardenias, a dark wind cutting sighs and shivers from the oak trees, raindrops splash and wet the streets so that heaven may be captured in iridescent puddles; my mouth remembers the exact juiciness of sunripe apricots and secret-scented guavas and hanepoot grapes tasting of coming home in the evening. But my country is not their country. How do I fit into these people's memories? They have changed with the contours of power and the perceptions of another order in this new land. We remember past one another.

A hand will be firmly wrung (do you still know who I am?). And the joviality of false recognition barked in laughter, a shoulder tapped or a cheek endowed with a peck (of course, what do you go and imagine there? how could I forget?). The slow minuet of spectres. Intense remembering has scorched one's memory. I insert too much meaning in the gaps and the cracks. Without knowing it I have become my own other. The heart has seasons which the trees will not colour.

We are somewhat nervous, shifting weight from foot to foot while long-lipping the sherry. Could it be any different? They are cautious (watching the cat from the tree, as Afrikaans would have it)—for how is one to get a grip on such a prickly fellow with his arrogance of otherworldly notions, his foreign clothes, his wife from somewhere overseas, the unpredictable bitter edge to his tongue? And I, how will I pretend there aren't deep scars left by the wet teeth of rats, nibbling that edge which demarcates the present from our shared youth? We must first get properly pissed together.

And yet it is soothing to be among the survivors, to exchange news snippets (from the kingdom of the dead), to grope with the best of intentions for that which may still be experienced as complicity. Let this much at least be celebrated! Here a magic formula had been proffered— even if the words and their meanings have since been obliterated. Here ordinary Boland soil became the flesh of sanctified experience.

Luckily the evening's events will be formally structured. In the dining hall there's a stage with two huge photo portraits of one's mother and father facing each other. The thought behind the gesture is generous, but maybe it would have been better not to have this confrontation. In our culture one is not supposed to cry in public. What, are we to be confused with Russians or Koreans? People have their mouths full of agreeable intentions they would like to splutter, of love and compassion and wanting to do good, and of pride and welcome home, and of please help us believe we will survive now that we stand stripped naked in the letting-go time; except that we have always been ungainly in matters of the tongue.

Good evening, beloved parents. Look, I lift a glass of wine from this deep earth resting in the dark night all around us. It was your town. You were the ones to be injured by what was bound to happen to me. It is of you that the birds congregating near the river still sing their stories. You are the ones welcomed back here where so many pious pricks and contaminated cunts, parading as the town's foremost citizens, ostracised you. The two of you, and the faded dreams in your eyes and the laughter of your lips and the buried pain of your nights, will be honoured tonight.

There will be a programme of poems, sometimes accompanied by guitar and song, respecting the necessary boundaries and measures. Listen attentively and you may still catch a voice linked to a given place, even though the protagonist has long since left. One's voice is not singular; it is the rider and one is the horse. Listen to it singing its own memory!

My words? Their words? Stutters and whispers in the dark. What does it matter whose words they are? Language is the live topography of a history of specificity. When the words are forgotten an awareness disappears. "To say is to make and to sing is to secure . . ." I am reminded of another popular wisdom that came to me in the shade of the pepper tree when I looked up to see the bobbing boots of my grandfather: "A glove of snakeskin makes it easy for the hand to catch snakes."

When people start shifting their weight from one

buttock to the other, there is at last a break. Freek and I head for outside, the bladder urgently needs to be relieved, and Kwaaiman follows suit. Just beyond the conversational circle of lamps we find privacy behind a low ring-wall, legs spread pleasantly wide. There's no room for Kwaaiman against the wall, he aims for what he takes to be a patch of lawn, unfumbles his fly, nature calls hurriedly, and the very next instant we hear a profanity and a splash. In the penumbra his shaven pate is a pale halo above the earth. What he took for 'lawn' turned out to be a fishpond overgrown with algae. Water gushes like shiny piss from Kwaaiman's pockets, the big fright sublimates his need. Right there behind the wall we bellow all of the evening's cropped-up tension from our bodies, vomitting wet moonlight.

You'll have to practise a lot more before you can walk on the water, Freek chides. Back at the table we still snort with mirth at the discomfiture of my brother, the short-arse Jesus, now sitting tight in his clammy suit smelling of old uncleaned duckpond.

Dinner is followed by a course of speeches. Christo, bosom buddy of former years, offers some witty and tender remarks. He tells of how he applied for permission to visit someone in prison, it is his duty to tend to lost souls, he is a man of the cloth, we will always have the poor and the witless and the orphan and the prisoner with us. But the security dogs with deodorant under the armpits uncover wet teeth and snarl in defence of their prey and their territory. Why does he wish to associate with a subversive? He is sorry. It is not intended as a political act. He has a family. He should have insisted, he says now. Lines snake down his nose and mouth, giving perspective to the forehead, and his body is heavier than in my memory. When my turn comes to express appreciation, his face has withdrawn to beyond the cone of light. It is flushed with dark blood just below the skin. Words have grabbed us by the throat. We thrash about in the ooze of some pond for the firm ground of shared remembrances. He was the most mischievous comrade I ever had and now the piety of the parson has given him a gaunt face. Blind Mr. Borges wrote: "The man who lies too often is bound to tell the truth inadvertently."

A small box is presented to me. Carved from the yellow Oregon pinewood of my mother's food larder in their old kitchen. Hand-fitted and smoothed by an aged cabinetmaker from Bonnievale. He must have beautiful hands. They say he is blind. Lined with green velvet. Empty. Full of meaning and echoes. What does it convey? The invisible heart. Rotted? Miraculously preserved? A nest for the firebird? Smooth the grain under fingertips.

(I remember the last time I held a similar casket, it was also the last time I'd seen Christo: it contained my father's ashes on that windy burial day in Hermanus when my friend's calm voice had to cover the ancestor with goodbye wishes, and the grief of the family with sonorous sounds.)

Night speeds to a close. We ingurgitate liquid words. My brother's jacket has shrunk, he has a wee frog in one trousers pocket. Photos are still to be taken. This one, of about fourteen survivors from the same class. Are they really one's contemporaries? In exchange for smaller expectations we have flourished in flab, and now we show our cracked and frumpish faces and our distended dewlaps and faint eyes to the flashlight. We with time blazed on hairless scalps, with abdomens slipped out of control . . .

Dark the giants' cathedral of mountains when we drive through the night. Mildewy the stars. Clogged the Milky Way. In a gorge there, one misty winter's afternoon, the sun is running late and evening rapidly floods the plains with ink, Christo and I on a hike lose our soulmate, the invisible Jansen whom only we could see, over the precipice he goes, carrying the rucksack of victuals and matches and dreams with him. Tonight when Christo spoke I could hear again the echo of Jansen's terrifying voice in the dying fall. The dead kick up such a racket.

THE ABSENT FACE

Diemersfontein, Sunday night. We partake of the evening meal with the farm's overseer and his progeny. From him we learn how it has become necessary for the district's farmers and their labourers to be grouped in security patrols, a kind of armed 'home guard' linked by radio, as protection against murderers and robbers. More people than birds are killed on the farms.

Not far from here the painter Hardy Botha runs an estate belonging to one of the big wine cooperatives. The farmhouse and the vaulted cellars have been transformed into living and working and exhibition quarters for sojourning artists, and more cottages added to accommodate visitors. But their haven of creativity was jinxed from the outset. People are stabbed, running fights light up the weekend nights like strings of firecrackers, dogs lie in the dust with ripped intestines, snakes fall from the trees, shots are fired through closed doors, firebugs commit arson and lovers commit suicide,

someone drowns in the dark dam from which the vineyards are irrigated.

Hardy met and married Kathy, the daughter of Alex
Boraine, an old friend from earlier times when the
struggle against injustice was noble. (Alex is now one
of the dogs of God; together with Archbishop Tutu he
chairs the inquisition called the Truth and Reconcilia-
tion Commission: misery and devastation and iniquity
and treachery and pain are staged before a bench of the
pure and beamed into the living rooms of the populace.
So that memory may be excavated, shaped, initiated
and corrected where needed to serve as backbone to the
new history of the new nation. Our earth is full of skeletons.)

Hardy the happy-go-lucky artist and the very blond
Kathy have a little daughter with cornflower eyes. Kathy takes the child for a stroll along the farm road. A
man appears from among the vines, he has a big stone
in his hand. Without a word he starts bashing Kathy.
He cracks her skull, he beats her face to a pulp, he
smashes her ribs, he breaks her arms. The agonised
screaming of the child attracts the attention of some
workers. The man runs away. Kathy's blond hair is dyed
a flamboyant red.

Doctors manage to save her life. She breathes feebly.
Her head will have to be rebuilt painstakingly, bone by
bone, and she lives between death and despair in a dark
room. She does not have a face to see with. The man is ap-
prehended after a while. He'd been incarcerated for murder and recently released long before his time was due,
and was now living in a nearby informal settlement. You
should understand that he is a victim of racism.

(This is not an isolated case: A gang leader in Guguletu was arrested five times in a row for five separate murders, and released each time on bail. The spirit of the new constitution intends us not to repeat the injustices of the past.)

Then, with soft rain coming down, we walk over to the main house for coffee with the owners. The guest farm belongs jointly to two of the richest families in the country.

The house is stocked with treasures, yellow-wood floors and benches of plaited thongs (*riempiesbanke*) are polished to a glow. Under a Victorian lampshade a striking portrait of a youthful beauty, probably painted in the London of the thirties, is positioned strategically. The lady is a stage artiste. How she must set the hearts of men aflutter! How they must rise from their chairs to applaud her charms!

She enters the drawing room, still as breathtakingly beautiful as in the painting (as long as she remains in the shadows), and sits down on the couch: the skeleton of a medium-sized bird with a haughty mask, elegantly folding herself against the cushions just beyond lamplight's inquisitive and cruel reach. Will you have milk with your coffee, my dear?

Her son has a beard and glasses. He speaks a sympathetic Afrikaans. He's a psychiatrist of the Freudian school: all that's lacking is the cigar and the cancerous mouth. Practises in London but regularly makes the trip out here to see to the estate's interests. One is being dispossessed in broad daylight. Have we heard about the senseless attack on Alex Boraine's daughter? He sees no evil, hears no evil, speaks no evil, but what does he think about in the dark room with his faceless child? There are so many expatriate Freudian analysts from this country living in London that they have started their own association.

(At this point one reflects that there must be a puzzling link between effect and cause, between the calamity of pathological alienation and white wealth, but one would have to let them all lay themselves open on a couch to caress the sombre secret from them.)

BACK TO SCHOOL

Monday morning at school we go through the proceedings of a prayer service (God is using the headmaster as a ventriloquist for his warnings) and the singing of the school's hymn, which I have long since forgotten. Also the two national anthems, merged haphazardly— this is a compromise of the new dispensation—the *Nkosi sikelele* part still somewhat bumpy. All the pupils, similarly clothed in coloured blazers, are gathered in the great hall. Among them quite a few brown and black faces. (We make a special effort to help them, says a teacher, because they often come from parlous home conditions.) The little ones fidget, the bigger boys try surreptitiously to feel up the girls' thighs.

I give my edifying talk about having faith in the future. It whizzes over their heads like a boomerang. They don't look up. The little ones fidget, etc. Afterwards there's time for a much freer exchange of thoughts with the senior pupils. How are they to address you? Sir? Uncle? Plain Breyten? We cover a wide field from past to future to where the two are knotted in the living memory thread of writing. Writing is always the present time finding its tense.

Coffee with the teaching staff. I am asked to sign a book in the principal's office. It is the story of my life in one slim volume. Now inspect photos of years gone by. My class in the final year at school.

I see a self-satisfied boy in his last presentation at school. Drooping eyelids and twisted smile, hair short at the sides, in a stacked wave on top. (From the back certainly an incipient ducktail.) He is thin, doesn't seem to be overly impressed by the solemnity of posing for a class portrait. Or pretends not to be. The future lies ahead, just beyond the light from the street, on the other side of the camera's glittering lens.

I cannot imagine myself inside the boy's head, I have no idea what his desires or fears might be. Does he know about wind? Does he use a deodorant? How long has he been masturbating? His lips are thicker than mine, his eyelids heavier, the head a narrow skiff (rather as if he wants to move ahead in the way of a bird), the shoulders less fleshed out.

The headmaster tried so hard to make everything go discreetly and pleasantly, and he has succeeded. Several times he shows me his friendly rose-red face. He says, I really don't see for what purpose: For every pied starling his own little pied starling has the whitest arse of all the pied starlings.

Mountains are clotted blue memories secreted from heaven, the heavens are blue too, the vineyards green, the houses white. The heart will always be a Boland bastard.

> my heart is in the Boland
> and nothing can profane it;
> it lies safely in its smallbox
> in white Wellington

MONTAGU

When we were little, our parents sometimes drove to Montagu to relax by the hot springs. It must be over weekends: women wear merry dresses, the men are proud as peacocks in white wide-legged trousers; they strike up a tune with piano-accordion, guitars, perhaps a banjo and a violin, and then dance in the dust.

The big flood of 1981, the 25th of January, springs as a brown roar of water from the inner reaches and folds of a knuckle-dry Karoo upcountry and rumbles away the bathhouses, the campsites, the towering shade trees in the ravine. Old men are found drowned among the driftwood, clutching at dead snakes.

People will tell you that the rush of cobra-coloured water chased up a cloud of dust as impenetrable as a prophecy from the Bible to redden the sun. It was the end of time. Uncle Koos Kock saved a young brown boy from the hissing torrent and swallowed so much dirty water in the process that he vomited uncontrollably and lost his dentures.

Koos Kock lived in Montagu but visited Bonnievale often. I grew up before him; as an infant I wet his knees. Whatever he touched would grow from the knobby green fingers, tough and sensitive like tubers always trying to burrow in the soil. He was in charge of trees and shrubs and flowers. At the rim of the town, against Noemnoembessiekop along the Barrydale road, he laid out a unique garden of *vygies (mesembryanthemum)*, the hardy indigenous succulents providing carpets of startling colour in the surrounding scrubland.

Flowering time in these parts is generally from July to October, except for the thorn trees which blossom in December, and then they are infested with *witbont dor-*

ingwurms (white-spotted thorn worms) which devour the flowers. One cannot spray poison—it would harm the smaller birds. The only solution is to go early in the morning before they start feeding, with burning newspapers on long sticks, and scorch the worms on the branch. In this way memory, too, is extinguished. Mesembryanthemum planted by the hand of man will not survive for long: they have an estimated lifespan of from four to ten years. But they love Montagu's dry and sweet soil.

Uncle Koos also brings into his garden Cape daisies, *suurknolle*, bietou, *madeliefies*, *koenie* trees, different species of thorn, guarri trees and all sorts of grasses. Even weeds: the resin bush, the Australian saltbush, *steekgras* (stick grass).

He collects many strange objects—earthen jars, small pitchers in which the old people imported red ink from distant lands, ancient wine casks. For some he devises his own labels: *Lawaaiwater* (Make-noise Water) and *Huismoles* (Home Fighting). He was once the proud owner of a *verneukglas*, a cheating glass—a specially designed goblet with a very thick bottom, pretending to be deep but holding little, used by masters of ceremony to propose endless toasts at receptions.

During our 1973 visit to Nomansland my mother took us to look for the old bald-faced gardener, but he was not to be found anywhere. Now all I have to go by is a juvenile souvenir of a tall stooped man wearing garish braces: he has deep blue eyes under bushy eyebrows, the toothless mouth is pleated in an eternal smile, the bald pate shines as if carrying the sun on a tray.

A man lives the life that is given to him, then leaves behind a wonderful garden and a thick-bottomed glass and the story of a chattering smile floating away on the froth of a flood. What more can one ask for?

Take the road from Ashton. It may be on a Saturday afternoon. In front of some workers' cottages a brown man will stand holding the hand of his small daughter. She will have ribbons in her hair and ribbons fluttering from her best white dress. The father will point out the passing car to the openmouthed child. He will not be all that secure on his feet.

A little further along three young maidens may be strolling towards the blue mountain fastness, they will throw coy glances in your direction, one will be strumming a guitar, their hips speak of the ancient knowledge of comforting. The road runs through Kogmanskloof, a defile between towering slabs of coloured rock. Inhabitants refer to the pass as the *Poort*—gateway, entrance and exit.

You may well cross a man coming the other way, purposefully pedalling a contraption built around a brazenly painted bike decorated with signs and pennons, he will be a nomad spreading the message of his life, the wind through the gorge whistling in his ears. The road will loop and you will see rearing before you a soaring stone cliff aflame with stained light, petrified tongues of creation, crushed symphonies, crevices and rifts burning with a mineral green, the yellow of holy robes, burnished reds, scabs of brown and ochre. Then you know you are about to enter Montagu.

Kwaaiman and Miriam's white-faced house perches on the flank of a ridge and looks out through two dark green apertures over Ou-Dam, the poorer part of the village. Just beyond the ringwall around his property the mountain takes over. Klipspringers—deft, shy, snorting buck which will whistle when startled—may come right up to the boundary. If you sit very still you can watch them trying to nibble on the leaves of a frutescent shrub. They have large, dark eyes.

His neighbours have visitors from the city, where backyards are cramped. They bring along two tame city peacocks which they allow to take a walk, to stretch their city legs, perhaps also to recompense them for the beauty of their shining in captivity. Let them for once go and release their desperate cries in open spaces! And then the birds do not come back. For two days three tipsy men stumble along the slope among bushes and stones, poking with long sticks, cursing most awfully: Haven't you guys noticed two fucking peabirds in the vicinity? Putting out maize won't do the trick; there is more attractive food in the wild.

When the mountain is as barren as damnation born in the mind of a Boer, baboons come to plunder my brother's garden. Not that he has much of a garden to speak of. These anthropoid beasts are knowing and impudent. Underneath a stone near the upper barbecue area there lives a rock lizard with a scaly orange-tinted body and a blue head. Whenever he raises his head on bandy prehistoric forelegs to hiss and puff out his chest, he looks just like a miniature dragon. There are geckos in the ceiling. They make small Khoi sounds at one another. At night they rummage through quiet loopholes of sleep with the noise of fidgety fingers in your ears. They also shit down the walls. They keep my brother and his wife awake and this doesn't do his temper any good. Ants emerge like streams of treacle from the earth and flow into the house. One works one's way up the marching columns with a kettle of boiling water until one reaches the fortress which is their communal memory. Some people do it with a spray can of poison.

But above all there are the red-winged starlings (*On-ychognatus morio*). It is said that Cecil John Rhodes, the foremost imperialist, had them imported from Europe—just as he brought the mynahs from India which devour everything along the eastern seaboard, and by now have spread inland as far as Johannesburg.

The birds multiply in flocks, worse than maggots in the carcass of a dead cow. In summer they are a blurred black fan before the midday sun: with beaks like greedy scissors they swoop to snip all the early fruit from the gardens. Each easily guzzles more than its own weight daily. Scouts take up position on the high branches (the troops are waiting in ambush among the leaves), watch the people and the crops, weigh up the ripening of the bounty and call the odds with a single prolonged fluted toot.

When one of them calls out, Kwaaiman tilts his head, gets up with a sigh, there's always something to be attended to, says: *Ja man, ja man,* I hear you, I'm coming, I'm coming. He will fetch the airgun, crack it, push a pellet into the breech. Often he hits the spy bird, a feather spirals to earth, but it makes hardly any difference—they are too tough.

Kwaaiman fights the baboons, the geckos, the starlings, the snakes, the crickets, the frogs, the ants, the plant lice and the neighbourhood's mongrels that come before daybreak to rip open the black plastic refuse bags. He will go down fighting. He has foreseen that things will come to this. One should have no illusions about life.

It is an unequal battle. His house is broken into, a few items of clothing and his electrical appliances are carried off. The thief is caught, he's still wearing my brother's jacket though he swears high and low by the gods of our ancestors both brown and white that he bought it in Cape Town on the Parade 'from someone who had a green hat on his head'. The thief is out on parole with a criminal record as long as his tattooed arm; there's not a prison whose black walls he doesn't know from the inside.

The case goes to court and my brother must testify. The accused is wanted for fourteen more burglaries. During recess the mother comes to Kwaaiman and cries a gnarled handful of tears from a wretched body, she really can't say what's the matter with the boy, didn't she thrash him abundantly when he was little? And, sir, can sir perhaps help me out with a small loan of twenty Rand, please, sir? The thief is found guilty on all charges and given a suspended sentence of fourteen months. My brother may buy back his belongings at the police auction.

That's nothing, says the prosecutor. A rural worker in the district commits murder and is sent to gaol. His family continues living in a smoke-cured labourer's cottage on the farmer's land. Every month they receive as family support an allowance from the State, this is the new policy. The murderer is given a remission of sentence, this too is policy, he qualifies as an ex-victim of racism, and long before his time he returns home, it is over and done with and now he must rest. The monthly allowance keeps on coming. The farmer drives into town, goes to see the prosecutor: What's this, then? The official explanation is that support to needy dependants of a prisoner is calculated according to the length of the conviction pronounced, irrespective of any remission or amnesty.

Again brother Kwaaiman's house gets burgled. This time his pistol is stolen. The knowing and impudent policeman comes to investigate. Was the weapon locked in an appropriate cupboard as the law prescribes? No? He goes to the chest where the weapon was supposed to be kept in safety, locks it carefully, yanks it open forcefully with screws and splinters flying in all directions, says: *Now* you have had a break-in!

They know who the thief is—but their hands are tied: the shooting iron has already disappeared into Zolani, the black township outside Ashton. Zolani is ANC-controlled territory, they blow away cops there.

The stealer is a youth who earns pocket money on Saturday afternoons carrying golf bags for local players. Through the mediation of another caddy my brother opens negotiations with the thief, to buy back his pistol. They agree on a price which will reflect the expenses and sacrifices incurred by the new proprietor. But then the transaction gets bogged down. The seller has no confidence that Kwaaiman will pay him as agreed. You just cannot trust these Boers.

MEMORY

Like starlings, memory devours everything. We live, we move forward as if travelling through a landscape, continually sharpening the eye—on the cusp of passing into oblivion—and immediately, constantly, inexorably the experience topples into the domain of memory. One instantly, constantly, inexorably turns to past tense. I am my own defecation. It is like being sucked out through the open hatch of an aircraft flying at very high altitude. It is like clinging to the crumbling lip of quicksand. We cannot live fast enough to escape the tongue of memory. It pronounces us. When we become conscious, it is already through the mouth of the past enunciating us in an attempt to catch up with the sound of time.

I tell Gogga: Just be patient and observe. Childhood lasts a very long time. It seems never-ending. Then the fullness of life is upon you in a rush, the middle years speed by, you are out of breath. Suddenly, constantly, inexorably, at last the flame has passed and now you have world enough to enjoy the good old days—your eye can eat the land and now you may imagine that past which you were too much in a hurry to live.

LITTLE KAROO

Montagu nestles in the most westerly corner of the Little Karoo—an oblong stretch of land between, to the south, the Langeberg and the Outeniqua mountain range (beyond those peaks lies the smoking ocean), and to the north the sheer mirror-mirage-message wall of the Swartberg behind which the big thirst-land, the Karoo, begins. The Khoikhoi call this region 'Kango', meaning "narrow plain between high mountains."

The climate is hot, slightly desertlike, with a nip to cold winter nights, but it is not as parched as most of the Karoo and less wet than the coastal strip. It is the natural habitat of ostriches and known for its vast variety of wildflowers, herbs and medicinal plants, as also for the baboons and leopards roaming the gorges where honey-coloured water flows from cool eyes in the earth.

The southern approach to the village, through vertiginous mountain walls of living fire, is the natural pass used by the Koekemans Khoi people driving their fat-

tailed sheep before them. Hence the present-day cor-
rupted name of Kogmans (or Cogmans) Kloof.

The present road was traced by Andrew Geddes Bain
in 1877. He wore a broad-brimmed hat to protect him
from the heat. At one point a tunnel had to be blasted
through Kalkoenkrans (Turkey Rock) because it blocked
access to the settlement. And ever since then a cold
wind has been blowing through the hole, one elderly
lady in town complains.

At the time of the Boer Liberation War, British soldiers—suffering from the sun, mosquitoes, fleas, dys-
entery, heavy khaki uniforms—built a stone fort on top
of this high rock with its hole. Phantom commandos of
bearded Boers might come galloping like a mirage from
the dust of the desert, the clattering hooves suddenly
resonating as an unannounced flood, Queen Victoria's
Empire must be defended! The fort's walls merge so
subtly with the surroundings, the shimmering air, that
you hardly notice its existence. The builders were given
this task because they had no stomach for the battle of
Magersfontein. Some soldiers carved their initials in the
village church tower. Their names and their stories have
long since been rubbed from living memory. On Sundays the bell clangs robustly from the steeple, but it
doesn't toll for them.

John Montagu, after whom the village would be
called, was the colonial secretary who initiated the
building of passes through the mountains to penetrate
the interior. The high one linking Wellington to
Worcester, built with the blood and sweat of four thousand convicts, is called Bain's Kloof Pass, after that same
versatile road maker who introduced wind to the Little
Karoo. (Bain was a soldier, a saddler, a trader, a hunter,
a witty newspaperman, a transcriber for the stage in

early Afrikaans of the adventures of a Hottentot woman
called Kaatje Kekkelbek, a collector of fossils and plants,
a farmer, a geologist . . .)

When I was still at school in Wellington I would
often go by bike to the top of Bains Kloof together with
Christo and Jansen. We would turn back and the narrow
road would touch the sky and then tip and plunge down
to the valley of vineyards. The three of us would pedal
furiously, wind streaming into our mouths. Then we
would free-wheel, whipping around hairpin bends,
whooping down the straights. Not just the wind made
us cold; we'd shiver with a delightful frisson because of
the mountain ghosts— all those unhappy chained prisoners who perished in hard labour. Like furtive flashes
their shallow graves under whitewashed stones could be
glimpsed from the precipices.

In these fertile valleys, boarded off by towers of blue
stone, the meeting between indigenous Khoisan tribes
and settler clans took place; from very early on cattle
farmers were permitted to rent grazing land in the interior—about twenty-five hundred hectares cost them
twelve Rixdollars. From 1699 they started moving inland, away from Company control.

By 1743, when Commissioner Gustav van Imhoff
stopped off at the Cape, cattle grazers had long since
established themselves in the Montagu area. In order to
rein in the outward movement and also "to protect these
pioneers from degeneration," Imhoff founded the Rood-
ezand church, serving the Kouebokkeveld, the Hantam
and the Roggeveld. Religious supervision would keep
the wild bastard farmers on the straight and narrow.

In 1745 a *landdrosdistrik* (magisterial district) was
proclaimed with Swellendam as seat. (The Company's
concern was to make the wayward people pay their

dues, rent, taxes, their *reconitie.*) The eastern frontier was now the Great Brak river. Montagu itself only became a separate district in 1895, seceding from Robertson, where a certain Colonel Caldicot Macsimilian Stevens acted as civil commissioner and magistrate. The locals called this Englishman Kaalgat (bare-arsed) Stevens.

The oldest farm was Roodewal (Ashton), attributed 1723 to Frederik Janz van Eeden *"om met zyn vee te mogen gaan leggen en wyden op de Roodewal"* (to graze and stay over). The next farm, now with acts of property, was De Goa, which became De Coo, which became Witkoo, and is today known as Langdam. In 1730 one Jozua Joubert was given full property rights, a condition being that he had to plant oak trees.

Language is made from the need to digest a new environment. I know this land, and yet I'm a stranger here. I have been away too long. I have to find a way of getting under its skin. One moves forward and backward over the soil, over the page.

What I want to write is the penetration, expansion, skirmishing, coupling, mixing, separation, regrouping of peoples and cultures—the glorious bastardisation of men and women mutually shaped by sky and rain and wind and soil. Particularly the soil where dead children make up new identities from old stories. And the light of sadness. I hear whistling bouncing off the rockface. Turn to look. Buck? Baboons? Wraiths drift up the mountain passes, smoke and fog . . .

And everywhere is exile; we tend to forget that now. The old ground disappears, expropriated by blood as new conflicting patterns emerge. People are trapped in the sad slanting light washing over the country, like ants in treacle. When the stories die we no longer exist.

In the latter half of the previous century, Kabbo, a Sam Bushman—captured in the interior, deported as prisoner to Cape Town—expressed this to his transcriber, Wilhelm Bleek: "Thou knowest that I sit waiting for the moon to turn back for me, that I may return to my place. That I may listen to all the people's stories when I visit them... Then I shall get hold of a story from them because they— the stories—float from a distance... For, I am here; I do not obtain stories... which float along; while I feel that the people of another place are here; they do not possess my stories. They do not talk my language... As regards myself... I am waiting that the moon may turn back for me that I may set my feet forward in the path... while I listen along the road, while I feel that my own name floats along the road; they—my three names—float along to my place... for this moon is the one about which I told thee... Therefore, I desire that it should return for me. For I have sat waiting for the boots, that I must put on to walk in, which are strong for the road..."

People die or start talking to the baboons or wander off into nowhere, following the moon.

After a while—we are now in 1786—the deserted farm De Uijtvlugt, lying behind the *Mond de Coghemans Cloof op de Cral*, was granted to Jacob François Joubert. Later still it was taken over at a lease of three pounds sterling per annum by one Pieter Swanepoel who'd come creaking and cursing over the crests from Wellington (then still Wagenmakersvallei, the Valley of Wagon Makers). He sold it in 1844 to Daniel S. Van der Merwe. And in the year 1850 van der Merwe measured out the village on this property.

It is thought that John Montagu himself—the indefatigable searcher probing for a Northwest passage, who prodded his horse for two thousand miles up and down the Colony in 1849 alone—came to baptise the urban settlement in January 1851. If so, he would have done it in a tent before sitting down to a meal in a house on Erf 35 which still stands in Long Street. The lamb tender, a great variety of vegetables, the wine somewhat heavy with sugar.

In the meantime more farmers obtained land in the district. People came and went. During 1880 Jan Daniel Pasqual was appointed guardian of the passage in Kogmanskloof at a place called Warmwater, to collect tolls there on wheels, harnessed animals, horned animals, animals under saddle, sheep, pigs, goats, ostriches, wagons without brakes . . .

Jan Daniel Pasqual was a born watchman; he was one of the guards keeping Napoleon Bonaparte at bay on St. Helena. Who knows why and when he came to the Colony?

One day, in Kloofberg, his young son goes looking for honey. There's a fountain in the mouth to the canyon, called "Almôrensfontein" (Every Morning Fountain), given that enough crystalline water will seep from night into morning to fill a daily bucket with its sweetness. The boy is lucky—by noon, as he starts on the way back to the tollgate over boulder and chasm, he is toting a canvas bag weighed down with honey.

The path is perilous, the grasses slicked with wetness, in a hurry he takes a shortcut. Then he slips, tumbles, chutes down a crevice, still clinging to the bag so that his arms get wedged too tightly for him to move.

A search party finds him early the next day in his stone entombment when his cries are already weak. Ants and flies are swarming over him, attracted by the split bag of honey, but surprisingly enough no leopard has yet caught scent of this hairless baboon. The rescuers try everything they know, all to no avail: even with a loop tightened around the shoulders they cannot budge him from his trap down the funnel.

The sun blazes overhead, the rocks tremble with heat, the men grunt and sweat and retire to chew on blades of grass in the shade, the boy's body is broken, shadows flow up the flanks of the mountain.

Until, his life bleeding away, he pleads: Dear father, please shoot me now. And with the last rays of the sun glinting on the barrel Pasqual squints down at his inert son, prays, wipes his eyes for a clearer aim, pulls the trigger.

THE VILLAGE MUSEUM

In Long Street there are two museums. One is the Joubert House, among the oldest habitations in the village. Here Paul Kruger, the president of the South African Republic (Transvaal) and his entourage spent the night during a visit to the area. One may see where he hung his silk topper from a peg, one can hear him clearing his chest and walking outside to spit out the tightness amid the strong-smelling herbs. It is just before the Liberation War. One is travelling the country to propagate one's cause and to feel the general pulse. The house is well restored and stocked with furniture and implements of a century ago. A tiny spinster is the caretaker, dressed exotically and twittering like a bird from foreign parts who doesn't quite know where to lay her egg. She warbles in the kitchen and flits from sombre chair to chair in the *voorhuis* (parlour).

Down the street the village museum is housed in

what used to be the Missionary Church. Shadows of cypresses paint sharp excavations in the whitewash of the outer wall, like quick breaths of pain.

Inside we visit the flotsam left by the floods of passing time—four-poster beds, latticed chairs, bead-embroidered clothes, handicraft and tools and knickknacks so typical of the pioneer environment, framed documents of legitimacy and portraits of the town elders making faces at history, memorabilia of famous events, banknotes no longer legal tender, mementos of well-known inhabitants, hearing-horns and yellowed newspaper clippings. A faded photograph shows an old gentleman with tie and hat sitting in a tree, naked heels drawn in under the buttocks, sun in his eyes, "a rare sighting of one of the strange but typical customs of our past."

This is where we saw the photo, that first time when we stopped to get to know the village. An oval gilded frame. A lady advanced in years looks straight into the eyes of the observer. She wears a dark frock with upstanding frilly collar, probably starched, and her eyes and hair are dark too. The museum's yellow-wood floorboards are honed to a sheen by time's passing steps. On the floor below the portrait there's a medicine bag scuffed from much use. A printed notice on the wall explains that it belonged to Rachel Susanna Keet, the midwife.

Some days down the road, we arrive late one night much further north on the edge of the desert in a town where my last surviving aunt lives, the one who has my mother's arms and upper lip and voice. Stars have already swivelled around the axle of dark hours. The town is really only a settlement of large plots, the inhabitants are absent, they have sailed away on the dry sea of a profound slumber, now and then a dog growls a grinding bark to warn off robbers or hungry lions lurking beyond the perimeter of faint light.

Despite the small night-hour Aunt Anna wants to entertain us with music. She accompanies her own singing on the family organ. She even insists that I should join in—How could you be of our family and not play any instrument? That harmonium used to have pride of place in our living room when I was small, it is a family heirloom from my mother's side, Kwaaiman is still trying to get it back. His fingers remember the feel of discoloured porcelain, he says. One day he will drive through the desert to fetch it, he says. Uncle Robert Meintjes, Aunt Anna's second husband, the life companion of her sunset years, gathers in an armchair his bones held together by skin, and keeps the beat with finger and foot. His eyeglasses reflect the light like coins put on a dead man's sight. Mosquitoes are being decimated by the ceiling's churning fan-blades; like wanton seeds they drift down on the floor. Another dog is telling off the night.

How is your health, Aunt Anna? No, the illness which will carry me away has not yet shown its face in my body, she says. Else I would have seen it in the mirror.

Then she asks about our adventures—where we have been, what we have seen. I remember our visit to Montagu and the portrait in the village museum which seemed so strangely familiar because of the way the dark lady fixed me with her eyes.

But don't you know who she is? It is your great-grandma!

Of course, I should have guessed! On every branch of my mother's family tree there's a Rachel Susanna

with wide skirts to cover the legs. My own sister was christened Rachel Susanna.

Little Granny Keet was the midwife and the sick-comforter of Montagu. She could be very severe (Aunt Anna recalls): when an unmarried woman was about to give birth she refused to help out the child until she was told the name of the progenitor. First the name, or else the shame. Afterwards she, your great-grandmother, would see to it that support was paid for the offspring.

She also took in the sick to look after them at home. And thus she died, to cut a long story short, just like that in her rocking chair one long night, while sitting up with a patient. The moaning of the wind could be a whimpering from the ailing guest. Sometimes the night is one enormous owl.

Early the next morning we prepare to continue our journey, a soft carpet of dead mosquitoes covers the floor, Lotus is outside with Aunt Anna touching and sniffing the roses in her garden, Aunt Anna has soft arms and a slightly nasal voice, I write a note to my mother to leave behind, to be taken along by Aunt Anna when it is her turn to enter that other night. By this token I promise to go back and look at the true history of Great-grandmother's story.

MEMORY

Where we stop to buy vegetables and fruit an ancient man shambles with his stick along the sidewalk. He must be well into his eighties, the hair of white wool contrasts with a shining black skin, the eyes are clouded, the stick is not very firm. When he sees me he smiles and greets by lifting an old but clean hat. He addresses me as *'baas'* (master). Master's hair and beard are now white too, he says, but *he* has known one ever since he was this high—a hand of brittle bones and callused skin is held at the hip.

A shiver runs down my spine. The old white-head's mind is clear. He's not confusing me with someone else. When he was but half-grown, he is intimating, I was already a grown man.

In the early morning a painter stands on a ladder to freshen the facade of the hardware store. Under one short leg of the ladder he has wedged a brush. I remark teasingly that he will have to choose: won't the ladder topple over if he takes out the paintbrush to continue his work? His entire face creases in one toothless grin. On his head he has a soft brownish cap. He is so privileged, he says, to be meeting me "from man to man."

At the hour of noon when the sun is white fire in the firmament I meet him again in the main street. Heat and the juice of dark dreams have evidently soaked into his body, he totters slightly on unstable feet. But he grabs my hand and squeezes it firmly, takes off his cap, looks me straight in the eye, tells of how he was hoping to see me again because of the big question which is weighing down his heart.

Who am I? He asks.

I must have faltered a response; what I wanted to get across was that he was certainly a pioneer South African, a veritable rainbow person, the full product of our painful past.

No, no—he continues; tell me now, what race am I? He continues holding my hand very tightly.

In the café where I buy the newspaper (they have a little of everything behind the counter and hanging from the ceiling: bicycles with tires already treated against thorns, jams, wood for outside cooking, clasp-knives, guitars, harmonicas from China because they are the cheapest, television antennae . . .), I am about to pay when another client enters. Early forties, glasses not clean, most of the hair gone, clothes somewhat slovenly, and from up close he gives off a sour reek.

He won't recognise me now, the man says while eyeing me. And again, this time addressing me directly from the side of the mouth: You don't know who I am. A reproach? I flounder, the world is such a big bailiwick, one gets names and faces and places mixed up.

His eyes dart in the direction of the cashier. My name is Hansie . . . And with muted voice: We were together.

Where? I want to know.

I'll tell you later, he says in a strangled whisper. But when he sees me preparing to leave he rapidly mutters the name of the prison.

UNCLE TAO

Adam calls from Cape Town to say he went to visit our mutual friend, Marthinus Versfeld, two days ago. We've known the old philosopher for many years, I always refer to him as Oom Martin or Oom Tao. In a guilty way I have thought about visiting him ever since our return to the country. He has been seriously ill for quite a while. This we all know.

Adam says he was invited into the study by Versfeld's wife. (I visualise that room: books smother the walls to the ceiling, on a shelf there's the only photograph in existence of Dirk Ligter, the legendary Hottentot out-law who could outrun any horse and who had the power to change himself into whatever shape he wanted—an anthill, a wanton lover, a shrub.) Marthinus Versfeld is lying on the cot in the study, a thin blanket over his legs, the embroidered smoking cap on his head, the eyes peacefully closed. The wife serves tea. They speak softly and take care not to clink their cups in their saucers so as not to disturb the deep thoughts of the recumbent old thinker.

When he leaves (Adam tells), he asks to be remembered to the philosopher and he delicately enquires after the real state of his health, we all know he has been seriously ill for quite a while. Oh, Versfeld's wife says, but he's been dead these last two days. We thought it best to leave him among his familiar books until the burial, which is tomorrow.

The epoch is full of bad news like a sky blackened by birds. We will miss him. We all remember the sermon he preached to the rocks on top of Table Mountain.

A few years ago I visited Oom Tao at his home in Cape Town. By then he had retired from teaching at the university, but he continued casting his philosophy in discussing *The City of God*, written by Augustine, or Plato's *Banquet*, or in describing how to build a house and where to situate the outhouse among fragrant shrubs, and how to sharpen a pencil. With great pride he showed me his roses and his herb garden.

It is an ancient custom in Taoism and in Buddhism to pass on a few well-used items before dying. Normally these belongings—the robe, the begging-bowl and the staff—are considered to be the insignia of an inheritance or a teaching transmitted to a successor, embodying continuation and filiation. From my heart to your heart.

One can be a follower of Oom Tao, though it will be

arduous, because he could be an irascible old man when the big wind curled a white tongue over the edge of the mountain, and full of contradictory expressions as well (Catholic, scholar, teacher, mountaineer, hunter, traditionalist, father of many children, aesthete, late bohemian, Afrikaner working in English, Taoist ...); one can at least learn from his humanism and try to be as close to the earth as he was; one can cultivate the wild heart as he did. But nobody can replace him.

On that afternoon he allows me into his inner sanctuary. He shows me some early books, and reminisces about Dirk Ligter. The two of us don't talk much. The study is full of shadows. It is a house of cats and dogs and the floorboards creak. He gives me a pocket knife, the finely honed blade still secure in its haft, it lies warm in his palm and then in mine, this takes him back many years to when his father gave him the knife, it is a Joseph Rodgers. He gives me a *gebrande kweperkierie*, a staff which he fashioned from a quince branch and hardened in the fire. He gives me a photograph of himself: sharp but naughty eyes, wild eyebrows like hairy caterpillars eaten by desert hermits, the toothless mouth with its dark and wet chuckles, skin like a parchment map of memory, embroidered smoking cap, a string used as a tie and held together by a ring with a stone.

After that visit we returned to Spain. It was summer. I would use the hooked staff as a *gancho* to bring down closer the branches for picking the figs when they ripened in autumn. One day, on an outing, we stopped by the side of the road to eat a watermelon. The rind was so tight with ripeness it cracked under the blade to reveal the sweet red flesh. When the eating is done I wipe my sticky hands before driving off—but forget the Joseph Rodgers on the hood of the car, and it is gone for ever. A few weeks later I cannot find the staff either—strange, I had it only this morning and now it has disappeared inexplicably, perhaps to be covered by brambles or weeds. Look high, look low. So only the photograph remains, sitting on the mantelpiece with a mocking and obfuscating expression. See? I have nothing to bequeath but emptiness!

I saw him one last time in Johannesburg during a conference on Afrikaans. He turned up late for the evening session, a bird of paradise on leave with his extravagant waistcoat and beaded cap. It is the bleak season of winter on the Highveld, frost whitens the grass. But tonight he has put around his neck a regular necktie of a vivid red colour: with a twinkle in his eye he pretends that he did so to salute me. Perhaps we know he'll not be with us much longer. When he enters the audience rise to their feet for a prolonged ovation. I get the chance to hold him to my chest. Then he makes a witty speech taking a few threads from his mind. He finishes by admonishing: *Opsaal*, Breyten! (On your horse!) Afterwards I ask him what he meant by the enigmatic instruction, he smiles and says—*Opsaal!* And don't fall off!

The stone church in Rondebosch is full for his funeral. On this Saturday afternoon sunlight is a yellow dust, birds twitter in the trees, from a distance comes the murmur of a crowd at a rugby match. The service reflects many faiths and customs. The presiding priest in green-bordered vestments intones Mass, a son reads a homily, a woman poet recites in Afrikaans a moving chapter from the Old Testament, a dark-skinned young man with long hair makes the air vibrate with a chanted

sutra. There are people present who normally never enter a church. Many cry openly. The coffin is taken away
down the aisle: on the lid there lies a big white pumpkin.
Also some bunches of garlic.

At the house there is tea and coffee and cake. Wine
for those of us who want something more substantial.
Then more pans of steaming food lovingly prepared by
competent brown hands appear from the kitchen. Conversation is like a flock of birds bumping against the
ceilings. There is no way out now. The floorboards
creak. In his study the black cap with the beads lies on
the cot. And an open book. A pipe with a blackened
bowl. As if he'd just gone into the garden to pee.

People mill around in the garden and inside in the
rooms and the corridors with the many shadows, all
looking for Martin Versfeld. So many that one cannot
see him. People from all stations and walks of life—
professors, clergymen, neighbours, modest brown folk
from the countryside, poets, family. His sons wear
brightly patterned waistcoats. An old dog doesn't quite
know how to keep out of the way, grumbles about hyp-
ocrites under his smelly breath, wonders what the old
man would have made of all this fuss, looks up at me
with a slow tail wagging: And what do *you* have to say
for yourself? A pilot takes hold of my arm and recounts
how he took Martin up for a spin in his small aeroplane,
how he had to dive low over the house so that the old
man could see his rose garden from above.

Later there will be music and the presentation of
texts. I am to read a poem. But we decide to leave, to
take the road back to Montagu with the sun setting
behind us. Oom Tao is no longer in the house.

BOLAND, A TRAVEL REFRAIN
(*at the memorial service for Marthinus Versfeld*)

behind us light faded in flares of trout and fire
   the dying must know about oceans and peaks
in their true temper and hour   earth
a burning thought when sparks in stubble-fields
escort the hearts of the pious
through a night where animals rise from hiding
   it was not yet night

we have the sun to track time and the moon
for fixed passages
   look, eclipse is but a passing shadow
   the dying knows sun and moon stars and tides
   his insight must enter unto the changes
and your countenance in the coffin
with the pumpkin on the lid
shone with ointment as you cleaved to deadness
   look, eclipse is but a passing thought   behind us
light dies in the season of shelters and shells

Boland autumn: how towering the sea and awash to all sides
to build attics in the waters
so that mountains may drink from the upper rooms
when the breath takes flight
and the dying learn by eye the shape of leaves
the silence of dust the moon
when the thoughts of ash bloom on the bone
where wind with fiery wings
spreads a tent in the sky

old sage, we celebrated you in a memory of garlic
and clay under the tent of your coffin
when the breath was taken away
for there was now neither guest nor host

and we so glad to be with you
in the hour of the waiting face
   it was not yet night
   look, passing is but an eclipse of thought
when you have to stare intently upon death

look how the eyes of the dying
know the teaching of leaves
on branches where birds lend their voices
to winds bringing messages of groves
from mountains with white fountains in the lee
and snorting buck in the gorges

your eyes went away: wild asses quench their thirst
bucks' hooves strike sparks from stones
rocks will be a shell for rock-rabbits
we forget the lovenames of stars   the trees are sumptuous
but unimaginable in the dark in the dark
you remember how to make people laugh
when they gather
   the dying knows
of oceans and seasons and hearth and fire
and moon and stars
clinging to true temper
with the incoming tide   with the incoming tide
you must go among people in many places and scorch
their languages with the tongue
   look, thought is only an eclipse of passing
   it was never night

but the earth's countenance shines again
all refreshed with ointment
   how strange it must be to be written by death
   to what avail if the road obfuscates
like fire over an earth burnt black
and there is now neither host nor guest?

through a gap in the mountains we left the Boland
   behind us light died in a tent of tongue and trout

through narrow passes over more ancient landscapes
shivering under the death of the moon
old agonist, may the frogs remember
may your eyes become sweeter year by year
brimful with the knowledge of silence
may your friends bring wine for the visit
for wine fortifies the heart in gladness
may the tent which you pitch remain steeped
in the scent of cedar and geranium and garlic and pumpkin
may the stars and the peaks and the passing
watch over you and your household
now and tomorrow and the dusk of each morning
and in the long waiting night of each one of those days

MEMORY

When it is day there are cloud-shadows skirting the
mountain like the banners of an army passing by. The
landscape unfolds towards the desert where all is black,
where sky trembles with heat-shivers, where seeing becomes a singing. But at night there is the stillness of
the living kingdom of death in a scintillation of eyes
overhead. The galaxy is a crop of white fires. Other
stars, as present as a dream vision with the mask torn
off, spell out all the declensions of innumerability. When
I was a small child we sometimes had to take to the
road. The point of departure was always the farm
tucked away deep in the dry infinitude of an interior.
The days would be sobbingly hot and bumpy and filled
with dust. The days would be like a reverberating
church full of sermons of damnation. And snakes would
want to nest in one's eyes. And my digestion would rise
up sour and nauseating in the mouth. That is why my
father thought it best to travel at night, early mornings

before the sky took on the colour of lemons, before blue rinds grew over the worm-infested domain of stars. The family car had a folding hood and we children were laid down on the back seats. I was instructed to count the stars so that I might not taste the dust and would not throw up.

Sometimes one has a premonitory dream—it drags you from sleep and beaches you soaked with a cold fear. We are in a scorched backyard in a Little Karoo town, several of us, with dust on our shoes. Suddenly a *boerboel* (Boer mastiff) comes around the corner of the house, we are trespassing on his territory, he viciously attacks my friend Adam, starts mauling him, shrieks splice the air in cords of raw terror, Adam manages to scramble through the fence with ripped pants. Then the dog turns on me, somehow both my wrists are now in his maw, I scream and scream. I have written a monstrous attacker which refuses to lie down on the page. There's a policeman present (is it his dog?) and I plead with him for help, rapidly according him promotion through the ranks from constable to general. The general has to prise the dog's jaws open to free my wrists. My palms are red. I still remember the sharpness of those teeth encircling my wrists like bracelets. Could there have been at heart some buried memory of being caught in a trap? It was Nietzsche who decided to call his pain 'Dog'. "It is equally faithful, unobtrusive and shameless, equally fun to be with . . . and I can scold it and vent my evil tempers on it." The dog, the dog! And somewhere I read about Frida Kahlo secreting through her wounded back and "smelling like a dead dog."

THE FLOWER HOUSE

Gogga refers to it as '*la maison à fleurs*' (flower house) because of the cascades of bougainvillea, flame-coloured hibiscus and poinsettia bushes, rose-shrubs draping the fences (the frangipanis are too young still)—but Lotus intends calling the house Paradys.

I have written often of this land as paradise, including in an ironical and bitter way, but this could be the first time that I truly return 'home.' Maybe I want to live here where it is unspoilt, where I can get a whiff of many herbs and flowers on the evening air, where wind has a voice, where the sun returns slowly to its resting place—clothing one mountain flank after another in garments of gold before slipping naked around the mouth of a canyon—where the frogs at night among the reeds of the river recite endless prayers to the stars, where a richness of birds flit and flutter and trill and squawk.

The air is still and dry, but with a sparkle. People often compare it to champagne. One becomes quiet here. Somebody in the village must be breeding carrier pigeons: when the flock heels and wheels in a scintillating whirr of light it is as if a bale of stone-washed blue silk is ripped simultaneously by myriad shiny scissors. That is the blinding sound one hears.

Death survives only in my own language, lives only in my country of origin, hides only under this tongue, moves only in the hand fumbling for the space of words and the detonation of metaphors. I have hollowed out this land with my writing—that too is now already a past, an unreadable archeological site of words, an absence, part of the big void. But language continues to sing, it rustles through the reeds which in earlier times were used to make flutes. Remember how Syrinx changed into reeds to escape from Pan, and how he made a flute to lick her thighs and thus evoked magical notes, birdflight, an orgasm? People celebrate life because death comes so easily. This has always been a violent country.

Because of the white wall protecting it and the lowly white construction with its flat roof, one has the impression of entering some North African casbah. A 'bauhenia' flings its branches heavy with purple-white flowers over the wall. There are butterflies like blossoms on the breeze. And the buzzing of bees. When wind brings rain through the Poort I hear all those butterflies and bees clattering on the corrugated tin roof of the cottage. Two gigantic and magnificent 'belhambra' trees, one growing inside the enclosure and one just outside, a male and a female (the latter is fruitless, the former bears seed clusters looking like small bunches of grapes), give a jungle of shade. They could be baobabs. Like slow, watery elephants they will in due time push over the house. Nobody knows who brought the trees to the district, maybe a long-forgotten exile or some young lover trying to create an illusion of paradise for his homesick bride. I imagine they originated from South America.

The riverbed in the narrow valley between us and the opposite mountain ridge is smothered by a sea of reeds. They say the invasion is due to the runoff from fertilised soil upcountry. If there were to be another flood the clogged river would surely burst its banks and spew a brown froth of destruction and death. But now the reeds constitute a refuge for red birds with black masks and yellow birds with quiffs, and provide a constant tide of rippling movement and sound.

There is often a dance of clouds, as if columns of silvery air are coughed from a circle of secret volcanoes.

Well camouflaged among the swaying reeds a cow is grazing. She is black and white. A woman and a little boy and a dog come looking for the cow, they bear feed which they will deposit in a drum by the river-crossing, the dog is black with white paws. Hook! Hook! Hook! the woman calls, the dog imitates her, the boy trots by her side.

When we go to visit my mother's grave in Hermanus, the seaside town where she is buried, something like the above scene will shake my heart. Lotus arranges flowers in a jar, I put my ear to the ground and hear my mother chatting, she was always garrulous, but the soil muffles the sense. As we leave the walled-in cemetery we notice a straight, elderly woman wearing layers of clothing, together with a small boy under the tall trees where mourners normally park their cars. They have their backs to us, they are too far away and too indigenous to this area for me to know whether they are brown or white. The boy is barefoot and he wears a coat too big for his size, his hands are lost in the sleeves. Sometimes woman and child stop and bend down. They must be picking something or turning over the stones. The woman has the serenity of all the world's protective care in her gestures. It is clear that the boy, staying close to her, is talking and perhaps singing in a bright voice ... Maybe he is telling her a story ... There's something so familiar in this memory ... Could it be? ... I remember the smell of her closeness, the softness of her arms, her slightly nasal voice. There's a tight ache in my chest ... Carefully I go towards them, the birds must not fly away, for what would I say if they were to stop and turn around? And if it turned out that indeed? ... What *then*?

But—instinctively?—they keep on moving just out of earshot. I want to cry: Wait! Wait for me! Mother! The past is a wind blowing away my voice.

A hundred yards further there is what seems to be a farmhouse surrounded by a wall. They enter through the gate. I walk faster. Don't lose sight of them. Not now. Now go into the courtyard.

They're gone. The house was clearly deserted a long time ago. On the street corner opposite live an old neighbor and his wife. His name is Jan. For a long time I call him *Oom* Jan, until he gently points out he's not that much older than I am. I still tend to address elderly people as *Uncle* and *Aunt* because I have been gone a lifetime and now unthinkingly see them as when I was young. Jan is retired, he used to work in Ashton's canning factory and has lost several fingers of both hands, sometimes he is still given dented tins of fruit or jam from the cannery, he has long since forgone all teeth or dentures, he wears shorts and goes barefoot, his full head of hair and his small beard trimmed to a point are white as the snow on Matroosberg in the winter, he has the body of a young man.

Neighbour Jan has a visitor. A *landloper*, a *swerwer* (a drifter) has turned up at his door, with ill-fitting hand-me-down clothes, a bulky suitcase and a loud laugh. (And a secret wish to stay.) On his way to a better life, he trumpets. Lady Luck is waiting for him at the next railway siding. What? He only spent time at the *pap-plaas* ('porridge farm', rehabilitation centre for alcohol-ics) these last few months to sit out the winter. Speaks with such a strong voice that the entire neighourhood follows the proceedings. Jan's very ugly, hoarse-voiced dog wheezes a bark, the canaries and parakeets kept in a big cage on the stoep screech and gaggle. Jan manages to convince the visitor to continue on his way to that appointment with Lady Luck. Don't you ever let her get away. There he goes loudly down the street, a man about to make his million in a promised land; soon he turns back for something he's forgotten. A commotion in the darkened house. Then, in a raspy voice, Jan's old woman, angrily: Beat it! Same to you, you old goats! Just thinking about getting it on! I'll have no truck with your goatish fancies!

Paradys is in Ou-Dam, the poorer part of Montagu, settled in 1854, known originally as Veldskoendorp after the labourers who lived here and walked in their home-made shoes to work in the vineyards of the white people around the hill; then Vrystaat (Free State), maybe for fugacious political reasons: we too once knew Utopia. After that it got the name of Ou-Dam, for there used to be a catch-dam where you go down to ford the reed-choked Keisie River when you come from Montagu proper.

Kwaaiman, perched a few streets higher than us, says the menfolk in this area have only three activities: drinking, washing their motorcars (dated jalopies which could have been imported from Havana), and beating their women. Brown people lived here cheek-by-jowl with the so-called Whites. Brown and White are only the momentary expressions of a subtle shading from before to afters. More poor whites moved in, some of them Railways pensioners settled by the government of the day. The inhabitants are modest, the houses humble with neatly cultivated vegetable patches under the fruit trees, flowers sharpen the light everywhere. It is still true that their capacity for drinking quietly but consistently, and the slow, elaborate, extended and persevering cursing which illuminates it, are unsurpassed.

One part used to be called Veghoek, the fighting quarter; another Poeshoek, because whores were known to flash their shop-soiled wares there.

A certain family celebrates a wedding, it is a Saturday afternoon, the house is crowded with quietly drinking and seriously cursing people, the father of the bride and his two sons ask the guests to stand out of the way, you damned lot of devil's offspring, and then knock down with crowbar and sledgehammer the wall between two rooms to make a place for dancing.

Our cottage was occupied by Oom Swanepoel and his wife and ten descendants. (One half of the dwelling, that is; in the other section lived two old spinsters with their goats and their geese and their chickens.) Sleepgat Swanepoel (Drag-arse) was his name, because he was a cripple and had to push himself along on a low box on wheels. Under the belhambra at the back, with its enormous, bulging, grey root structure like young elephants half-immersed in the soil, he kept his donkeys and a cart. With great difficulty he hoisted himself on the cart to clip-clop into town, but upon arrival in front of the hotel in Bath Street (it is told), he was off and into the bar and up on a stool like a slab of wet soap.

When clearing the garden I come across a tiny horseshoe probably shed by a long-dead donkey, and we have it cemented into the wall for luck.

"Since then the name has been changed to Montagu West and a different type of person lives there now— to a large extent anyway." (This information I glean from a letter in the local museum when I start looking for traces of my great-grandmother.) "In the 1880's it was a favourite haunt of the young boys. A rare type of canary was found there, also the bushes on which they used to feed . . . Both canaries and bushes have since disappeared completely from the district. There also used to be large patches of *koekemakrankas*. The inhabitants of Montagu West of that time had a most fascinating name for them (which unfortunately I've forgotten). The children used to love eating the *koekemakrankas*, which are also now very rare in the district ... (Your husband will explain to you what a '*koekemakranka*' is.) My father told me all this ..."

The *koekemakranka (Gethyllis afra)* is a shy pod- or finger-like medicinal plant filled with small seeds and with a peculiarly strong smell. It was known and used by the Khoi of old, farmers kept it in brandy as medicine, but it is now practically extinct.

MEMORY

A terrible accident happened to my friend Professor Adam. He returned home from university yesterday and found his dog Nietzke chewing up a manuscript he'd been working on—apparently all about the "silent voices" in the colonial discourse. It couldn't have been too thick a document! In all the faculties, do-gooders are now trying to listen their way back into the past (*like me*), but the problem has always been *our* ears, not *their* voices. Anyway, he fought with the dog and his hands were bitten so severely that both had to be amputated.

Why does this information (from Kwaaiman) bring back the memory of other dogs barking down the years? I remember a hermit who lived in a dilapidated shack near the big river on the Jonkers' farm. He was very ragged and out-at-arse, ill-used by sun and rain and wind. He had the foul smell of a rotten dog. Nobody could tell whether he was white or brown; when you are poor enough these distinctions fall away with time. We children were a little jumpy with old Arthur Rommel, although we often teased him and then ran to hide. He was forever walking alone in the hills, talking to himself with his hands. Sometimes he howled and snarled, with foam flecking his chin, as if he were poisoned. Sundays he came with a feather in his hat and a stick in his hand to make noise outside the church hall where we were having the weekly service. We young rascals even made up a rhyme about him. The original 'rhyme', I imagine, would translate something like this: An outlawed beggar lives near Vrotkop and shouts outside the hall: "Who will make me a bid? If there is man, there can be no God. If God exists then we are fucked." Then he laughed and pulled his meat right there in public on a Sunday morning! One day he went down on his knees, his trousers smeared with semen, and said: Didn't I tell you the self is poisoned ratfood?

HEARTLAND

I left here young and my childhood was spent in other places, living from the many travelling trunks with their false bottoms. Neither my father nor my mother ever told stories about their past. Why do I then feel at home among these hills, along the slopes of this river? Does one only later decipher the gestures and the songs of the ancestors?

I recognise how much I resemble my people. By now I have my own false-bottomed suitcases stuffed with time, with wrinkles and with flatulence, so that I may be the equal of the *oumense*, the old ones, all those I used to call 'uncle' and 'aunt' . . . I bear the scars they had when they were as old as I am now.

On my father's side there is a birthmark as big as a fifty-cent piece journeying from one generation to the next. Oupa Jan has the dark brown stain just below one ear; Father has it in the fold of his right arm and when he flexes his muscles it grows in size; my eldest brother, Bruinman, has it on the upper thigh, as if he'd spilt coffee in his lap. I don't have it and neither has Gogga, but Bruinman's son, Dirkie, has it sitting on his wrist, black and puckered and furry like some dark-faced watch without time.

Because we are so much alike on the outside—in a glance from the mirror or in the opening of a door or the tilt at which a cup is held I detect a familiar gesture—and since outside and inside hang together and cannot be sundered, I now start experiencing my dead ones from within. Is this not what life is about: to leaf through the book of yourself and come upon known stories which you've never read before?

Thus I recognise as through a glass darkly, which is memory, their memory, the light on these scenes, the flash of a stretch of water in the river's turning, the breeze of nostalgia through plumed rushes and the slight shiver of leaves in blue-gum crests, the exceptionally slanted angle of rain-stripes, the exploding blotches of red canna which hurt the breath, the odours of this veld with its bushes and the main street's dusty smell, the shape and the bulge of knolls and the indistinct refrain of distant blue mountains like curtains soon to be raised on a play, a play I know from somewhere by heart, the partition of clouds, the pattern of ants in fighting formations, the sound of sun on stones. This must then be the true "country of the heart."

I walk and sit like these people, and speak the same sounds. If I used braces my trousers would also look like a bag of onions hung from the rafter and if I wore a hat it would also have been tipped over one eye. When we come around Vrotkop and look down upon the pattern of vineyards, the shade of prickly pears merging with the soil, the movements of squat bushes, then I know I'm looking through my grandfather's eyes. And when I put a blade of grass in the mouth to chew I taste my father's spittle.

Heartland: Montagu, Robertson, Stormsvlei, Wakkerstroom, Bonnievale, Swellendam, Riviersonderend, Bredasdorp. Areas known as *Overberg* (Beyond-the-Mountain), the *Rûens* (the Ridges), *Bossiesveld* (Scrubland), *Klein Karoo*. Tissue of words, maps fixing experiences and 'knowledge' folding in upon themselves. Beyond the inner circle: Riversdal, Stilbaai, Waenhuiskrans, Struisbaai, Agulhas, Nagwag (the cluster of farms where my mother was born), Elim, Protem, Klipdale, Klaas Voogds, MacGregor—and then over the Hex River mountains to the more classical Boland of Wellington and Paarl...

Perhaps the Boland is more settled, more durable. There is movement too; the 'Upper Country' may even be considered the cradle of change, many traditions and usages intersect and knot there, but all within a more privileged space. 'Culture' means white homesteads on well-ordered farms. The class distinction between white and brown is harsher. Slavery bites deeper, becomes more rooted, it even flowers in jollity and carnivals.

Why do I then want to be on this side of the blue mountains in a barren paradise? Maybe because of the simplicity and the poverty. And the reach of some of those emblematic names: *Wakkerstroom* (Stream-of-Consciousness), *Nagwag* (Nightwatch), *Stormsvlei* (Marsh of Storms), *Riviersonderend* (River-without-end).

For here, on this side of a blue barrier tipped a breathless white in winter, lies buried the seed germ of my going away, which is a mongrelisation. Absence has roots in this border area between the somewhere of a Boland and the nowhere of a good-for-nothing interior. People are the products and protagonists of mixing. As with people, so the tongue: our shimmering plough of survival under its far spurt of purple dust, that which only in the turning over of sods will become plough-share, blade of exploration, lines which permit us to reach a settlement with what must be conquered, where the world, naming by naming, could get its face. These people, this language, are without defence. They will be absorbed or defecated. They have no pretensions with which to protect themselves.

Yet: within the confines of these blue walls one can see the still smouldering campfires of the *trekvolk*, the eternal migrants. On towards the great transformation, the *groot andersmaak*. It is in the congealment during the shift of the prism, in the last illusion of meaning during the fragmentation, in the half-closing of the eye against the smoke, in the transition of one essence to etiolation (and later another essence) that the ache is naked.

The present tense is only a constantly expanding past. A topography; the momentary and fragmentary fixing in words of letting-go time.

(*Let us have a minute of silence there, you devil's spawn!*)

DOG GONE

After a decent interval I call their home. Mercy answers. She has a high-pitched voice. I don't know how to broach the subject of Adam's missing hands. And how is he? Oh, very well—she says. Happy among his books in the study. Am I imagining a darker tint to the tone of her response? He's right here by the telephone, do you want to speak to him?

His mouth is full of laughter as always. Carefully I prod the incident with the dog. Oh, that? He chuckles some more. A minor debate with Nietzke, she's only a puppy, but boy, are the teeth sharp! I'm trying to teach her to play cop and pickpocket, the way we saw it on the rugby field in Bonnievale, remember? And she bit him without intending to. The dog had a bigger fright than he had. No, nothing serious. He now has a neat little scar on one wrist. To go with the bracelet that I gave him as a souvenir years ago.

And the manuscript? What manuscript? he wants to know. There's a stretch of silence. You mean the story about the dog that swallowed the document? Where did you hear about it?

This is the way he tells it. He says it is an elaborate joke making the rounds in Cape Town. The chief dogs of God, your friend Alex and Bishop Tutu of the Truth Commission, are trying to get the National Party to admit to responsibility for the atrocious years of repression. Afrikaner commissioners and lawyers (with freshly rinsed and absolved souls) are chasing the party's spokesperson up the tree of their own selective amnesia.

Ah, to be a Truth Commissioner! Look high, look low! Watch out for the snake in the tree!

The story goes like this, says Adam: The spokesperson of the National Party submits that his organisation is not at all the evil entity it is now made out to be; no, it was indeed their intention many years ago already to abolish the whole system. They had a carefully worked-out plan: Release all the political prisoners, legalise the banned liberation organisations, organise countrywide elections under international supervision. Given the sensitive circumstances, it has to be a highly secret project until such time as all the ministers and generals agree to it. A junior minister, one Jacobus Oberholzer Benadé, is (as decoy) the only official entrusted with a complete set of proposals. In light of what then occurs it is ironical that Benadé, as minister of local affairs, is ultimately responsible also for keeping the sidewalks clean.

There is to be a meeting of the full cabinet plus the National Security Council, on a Wednesday, where the plan is to be unveiled and certainly (given the traditions and the structures of authority) approved. The minister has a dog, a *boerboel* mischievously called Botha. Afrikaners have a sense of humour. A running joke has it that Benadé's dog is a crocodile, because of its toothsome grin! So here we have on this big day a nervous minister, burping as he rushes out to where his chauffeur is waiting in the official car at the kerb. In his briefcase he carries the document that will change the face of history.

Botha gambols around his feet, slobbering over his pants, getting in the way. On the pavement Minister Benadé slips on an uncollected dog turd. His head hits the flagstones so violently that it cracks open like a ripe watermelon. Botha, still thinking it's a game, grabs the briefcase in his jaws and runs off with the chauffeur in pursuit. By the time the chauffeur returns puffing to the car, he finds the minister dead, the blood coagulating around the dog shit.

The dog is hiding at the bottom of the garden. He growls when they try to take away the briefcase—is it not his master's? In any event, it has been chewed to a pulp, the contents devoured. (It is known that Jacobus Oberholzer Benadé, suffering from heartburn, was conveying specially prepared sandwiches among his papers.)

Of course attempts have to be made to retrieve this utterly important document which, now so many years later, will exculpate the National Party and remove the politically motivated aspersions of petrified racism. Does the commission know that, with infinite care and patience, dogs can be taught to speak? A Russian expert in the field is secretly brought to this country. He is to elicit (through regurgitation) the information from Botha. At the very least some proof of change of heart can and must be produced.

Meanwhile opinion among the rulers is also changing. Some detect the finger of God in all this. They feel besieged, are going to fight to the finish. No more history. No more Mister Nice Guy. History is just dog droppings.

The Russian continues his efforts, probably with the instruction that he should now plug the leak of momentary weakness, but for whom does he really work? One knows that the Soviets mothered the ANC. Could it not be imagined that *they* managed to get hold of the information, now carefully hidden away and stinking in one of their briefcases, which would have made of the National Party a partner in democracy?

Botha dies. He has sired some offspring, though not

always coupling with much discernment. Thus the spokesperson of the National Party wishes to call before the commission as potential witness (to be interrogated by Comrade Fyodorovitch, now known to be teaching phonetics at the University of Stellenbosch) this Chihuahua, Flaffie, despite its bedraggled appearance a direct descendant of the well-documented Botha.

DISMEMBERMENT

Adam says they finally know what happened to their neighbour up the road. The old man was as quiet as could be, never hurt a fly, a retired insurance employee, wore a hat when out for his regular evening stroll, seemed not to have any family. Adam sometimes spoke to him, the old man had a particular interest in medicinal herbs indigenous to the western Cape, he even knew some of the Hottentot names. Then nobody saw him for a long time, there were no lights in his house but the front door was ajar. The power equation has changed in the land, people keep to themselves, nobody admits to having opinions except via anonymous letters to the newspaper. Today an overworked, barely literate, gum-chewing detective comes to ask a few perfunctory questions (Nietzke has to be locked in a back room). The old man's partly decomposed corpse has been unearthed by dogs in a shallow grave near a squatter camp close by the international airport. Robbed of shoes, money, watch and eyeglasses. There was a hat with him in the earth. (A black hat? Adam asks. Yes, says the gumshoe—and this permits the identification.) His heart and testicles have been hacked out, presumably to be used as *muti*, magical medicine. The eyes too are gone, gouged from their sockets. So that he cannot look at the Other. This is what gets him, says Adam—the eyes. Glasses he can understand, but why the eyes? The old man was practically blind.

MEMORY/FATHER

He was gone, my father, and his absence worried me. I know he's been dead a long time but this is no excuse to go gallivanting, anything might happen. Today the sun shines, filling passage and parlour with gold. He must have come back during the night. I didn't hear him come in. While I look by the front door to see if any mail has been pushed through the slot, I notice him from the corner of my eye, my father. Morning light paints his face an old yellow colour, he seems exhausted, the skin all wrinkled. He greets me with a tired chuckle. What good will it do to remonstrate with him? He won't listen to me, I can't tie him up in a tree, he is my father. Today he is stark naked. How on earth did he get to be this thin? Who stole his clothes? Behind him, as loyal as a shadow, is his body-companion, the black youth who never says a word and goes with him wherever he goes. The dead always go in pairs, otherwise there is no proof of existence. He must be dumb, he never talks. The youngster holds up a mirror. I know I must open the window to the parlour because it smells of burnt flesh in here. My father has a clothing iron. He is busy carefully ironing out the pleats of his face. There's a sizzle and then thin smoke. His eyes are very apologetic but also so very tired.

RESTORING PARADYS, AND
OUPATJIE SNOEK

Where the road swings away from the outside gate to Paradys, on a small plot of open land overlooking the river with its rhythm of reeds, and beyond that the valley floor (called Lovers Walk) narrowing to the left towards where a solitary farmhouse guards the entrance to Bath Kloof and Donker Kloof, there the enormous belhambra tree grows. Call it the singing tree. All day long a whole vocabulary of bees will buzz among the branches, humming the entire tree with their hungry sound, so that one may hear it from quite a distance with eyes closed.

In the old days it was known as *die geselsboom* (the talk tree): on Saturdays neighbours gathered in its shade, made themselves comfortable on the huge roots providing bench and stool, filled their pipes and *thucked* the cork from a bottle, to discuss the week's gossip and whatever else needed to be chewed and inspected. The bees now echo those voices which have floated away. ("Then I shall get hold of a story from them because they—the stories—float from a distance.")

Higher up, a thick branch still bears the signs of having been the perch of a *boom-Boer*. The bark is worn smooth and a heart is carved in the flesh: with time it grew its own lips. From there one could keep an eye on the snakes, of which there are many, attracted by the swinging nests which weaverbirds plait in the thorn trees near the river, and with the other eye keep watch on the mouth of the canyon, from which rampant floodwaters may yet hiss and shout.

A thickset gentleman with a red face and a head bald and polished except for some reddish fluff, shorts and socks to just below the knees, comes to ask if he may look around. He has a perplexed look. What does *meneer* see in this old place? Why do you want to come and live here? Maybe something important escapes him. His name is Swanepoel. He was born right on this spot; with many brothers and sisters he grew up in the shade of this very elephant of a tree. When branches speak of wind the donkeys will sing along in harmony. Married? Yes, *meneer*. Got a decent job. Finally could move away. Bought himself a slip of land over on that side and had a *proper* house built. Now here he sees people, city folk to boot, who ought to know better, intending to stay. Whyever?

Freek brings over a team of builders from Kleinbos to restore the cottage. They arrive on a lorry loaded with implements and building material. The reeds for the ceiling they will go cut in the marshes on Pietersfontein, a farm outside town in the Keisie Valley. When they have unloaded all the trunks and the tools a small old gentleman is uncovered. This is Oupatjie Snoek (Little Grandfather Barracouta). He is fast asleep, curled up like a withered fetus or like a shell listening to its own susurration. It is Monday and he must still sleep off Saturday night's drunkenness. How can one remain unconscious for that long? By drinking huge quantities of semisweet wine very quickly on an empty stomach.

Gently the builders lift him off the lorry and lay him down in the shade of the house. As the sun moves through the spheres, so they will shift Oupatjie Snoek to keep him in the cool strip where the rays do not penetrate. Tomorrow he will wake up and know neither where he is nor how he got here. Then his mates will remorselessly make him do the hardest work.

Nights they all sleep in one room. They have brought

along a television set and the bluish light of empty images conveyed to them from America by the new South
Africa flickers over their faces. Oupatjie Snoek shyly
smiles at me with a toothless mouth. He hasn't seen me
before; I must be part of his dream. I exchange small
bits of talk with the men. They are intrigued by this
foreigner from abroad who speaks their language.
Apools (braver than his fellows and egged on with much
teasing laughter) will eventually venture some questions. And over there, in Europe, are there brown and
black people too? The follow-up query will come later
in a more roundabout way: Are they also discriminated
against? They shift uncomfortably, laugh down their
chins behind their hands, shake their heads in wonder.
Tonight they will cover their heads with their blankets.

Cyril is in charge of the team. He is tall and sinewy
and taciturn. Day and night he wears a seaman's cap
with anchor and braid as blue as his eyes. On the roof
he stands straight and strong. When not working he
will sit by himself, whistle a song and whittle a stick.
The song becomes thinner. During the week nobody
touches a drop of alcohol. But on Saturdays one must
bring up to the house several jerricans of the local swee-
tish wine. Montagu is known for its fine Muscadels, and
the other vintages of the region have more body as well:
the soil is deeper, the air more arid and the sun hotter
than in the Boland. Then Oupatjie Snoek's thirst rises
up like a primeval flood in the veins, in his head he hears
the songs and the stories of the old people, he floats
away to where cattle are family and magical animals live
bellowing under the earth. He will be away until Tues-
day.

Lotus and I are living with Kwaaiman until such time
as the ceiling of fresh reeds has been laid and we may

move down the hill to Paradys. When that is done the house will be filled with a warm smell. Kwaaiman's neighbour, one street down, is Koos Karretjie (Little Cart). Everybody knows him by this name because he is the local taxi driver. He recovers and repairs only one model of motorcar, Opel sedans, of which he has four, all painted the same blue with his name on the door, all equally decrepit with similar dents and bumps. Only one runs at any given time, the others are kept in reserve to be cannibalised for spare parts. When he starts up the valid car with a stutter and a cough, a tangy, purplish smoke drifts up the hill. The carrier pigeons have an excuse to unzip the skies. But mostly his wife must help him push the vehicle to life.

He is a stocky man, always in shorts and barefoot, the sparse hair watered down. I have never seen him smile. His rages, the bursts of inventive cursing, the prolonged sessions of beating the wife, can be heard all over the neighbourhood. In the evenings they sit on the stoep to enjoy the respite of a cooling day and watch the pigeons return like second thoughts, placid and silent, the beater and the beaten maybe equally tough, comfortable in their morose togetherness. The wall around their low, iron-roofed house is painted a shocking pink. In the wall are inserted whitewashed wagonwheels. One sees an ancient plough and the model of a Karoo windmill peeking from the courtyard, both painted silver and mounted as totems of the past defying the future.

Living next to the Karretjie family in a house made nearly invisible by an overgrowth of vine, there's Ingrid Welz, the widow of the Austrian painter Jean Welz, who emigrated to South Africa in the 1940s. He painted interior scenes, still lifes and nudes bathed in a forgotten

European-memory light. Jean suffered from tuberculosis, it was thought the dry Karoo air would cure his lungs. He died an old man. She is of Danish origin, careless with the treasury of paintings and silver cutlery still in the house, bent double with extreme age like a half-closed jackknife, patiently looked after by a spinster called Carol who has a talking dog and an out-of-sorts house of her own a few streets further down the village.

Late on a Sunday morning an old refurbished American Chevrolet with tailfins and chrome stops before the house across from Kwaaiman's. The car is praying at the top of its voice: the radio loudly blares a Sunday sermon. Two young men get out—all fired up, mind cowboys, hair glued stiff in ripples, combs tucked in their socks. After a while another passenger emerges with difficulty from the back seat. The father. He is a tiny cock sparrow, his hat sitting at a precarious angle on his head. But very dignified as, helplessly and blindly and silently inebriated, he fastidiously navigates a swaying lurch past a yapping little dog to the front door whose knob keeps eluding him.

A wan-faced elderly Englishman walks his two tiny pug-nosed pooches up the street. He wants to engage me in conversation. Complains bitterly about the municipality not keeping up the sidewalks, discriminating against pets, particularly his, not properly providing storm drains for torrential waters when the clouds break beyond the Poort.

He's heard it said that I'm the writer. Is it true? He'd like to have my expert opinion on a manuscript he happens to have ready for publication, to wit, the life of the mother of these lovely two companions, complete with photos, including one of her grave. She was no mean dog, sir. His head trembles and his eyes are weak with water.

And maybe I can give him some advice? He's a lover of music, see, in happy possession of a beautiful collection of gramophone records, you are most welcome to come and listen, among them a few in Afrikaans, songs of Jurie Ferreira for instance (he's referring to musicians who were popular forty years ago), and now some of his English friends in the village are asking—How dare you have that Afrikaans trash in your home? Is he wrong, pray? Isn't music just music? Must he now be ostracised?

Then, speaking of Ou-Dam (which is where he lives just like we do) and suddenly switching to Afrikaans: *Net arm mense bly daar. Hulle is almal bywoners!* (Only poor people live there. They're all sub-farmers, or squatters.)

The neighbors object to festive sounds floating over the white wall around Paradys. Must be a drunken orgy in there, they assume. Soon there will be violence and thieving. Murder, for sure. The police come to check. Turns out, however, that Cyril and his men are singing psalms and hymns, the harmonising punctuated by vigorous praying. One has to speak up because God is very hard of hearing when it comes to the humble petitions of brown people. Oupatjie Snoek sings the loudest and the sweetest; he has the most pain to bring to our Lord. Especially the headaches.

When they are done and the lorry is all packed with their belongings for the return journey to Kleinbos, they come to say goodbye. The men are dressed in their best going-away clothes. Oupatjie Snoek is as sober as a church sacristan with long lips that have no memory of Saturday. Cyril takes off his seaman's cap, for the first time I notice how pale his forehead is, and solemnly wishes me and Lotus all the best for our future life. The men shuffle their feet and clear their throats in amen. May the good Lord keep watch over you and your household, all the days and all the nights of those days. They have had to rebuild the chimney to give it more *sluk* (swallow, meaning throat or draught), it was smoking into the house. Now it has the fresh warmth of newly cut reeds. They close their eyes as a farewell prayer is said. Then a final hymn of sadness and they're away with much waving. Oupatjie Snoek doesn't know where they're going, but he is happy to go along.

A neighbour comes to explain that it is a great pity, it wasn't he who complained about the noise, such Christian people, even if they are Hotnots, why, he doesn't have a telephone to call the police with, it was that other Englishman living on the corner.

HOUSE POEM

the house lives well:
each corner is twined in clustered bougainvillea,
flame or intimate coral of mouth or the popish
garnet-laughter of satin rubbing
their colours against the eye,
baked mudwalls store
the sun's white scripture
and on the iron roof you hear the slitting steps
of laughing-doves scraping their nails,
or at times that other
sweeter alphabet
when raindrops fall,
but usually the moon-sheets of light
glow slowly over the hills,
sunbirds sway from calyx to sheath,
lemons and apricots yellow with the heat,
finches' nests give head to the wind's
rustling breath through the gulch

from thorn tree to pomegranate bush
not yet ripe,
our bed has the rhythm of dreams stolen
when frogs in the marshes moonthematically
break wind
and their palpitating hearts

murderers hide in the mountain fastnesses
where rocks are spurting fire and poison and ore,
of the old people are left only
names for rivers and peaks and passes
like sparks and stars and live coals
and blackened caves
with carving stone and shards of absence
washed by passing,
all the aromas which they smelled
and the light weight of objects and landscapes
lit up by their eyes

of the old people are left
dreams harvested and dried
when they planted shrubs against the forgetting
of another continent, beyond other currents,
sailings and journeys and states and deaths,
other heavenly systems with insects as gods,
when their mouths learned to fit
the spittle and the fuller pliancy
of the language of beetle and ash,
the hollower things of the throat,
and vowels like ringed exotic birds

are left a furtive laugh in the dusk,
the rushing fleece of satin frocks,
our handed-down slant of standing against the view
while waiting for the light,
but usually the moon glistens like the salt
of stars over the hills

days already the lookout-tree
guarding over the outer wall
like the elephant's other memory
is one big buzztevity of bees

you listen to the anthem of time
with feathers in the throat

our bed has the rhythm of dreams

MEMORY

The memories which I collect (the memory which I collect) are like periwinkle shells to indicate the spot where the dust is buried. It makes it easier to find myself.

I remember that people travel at night in order not to know about the dust. I have not forgotten the vomiting. I remember my two elder brothers. (Hartman, the younger sibling, must be too small to leave a mark; Rachel is not yet born.)

But I have no clear image of myself. I don't know what I'm looking for.

In the house where we reside (which I do not remember) there lives a big, tame white parrot. It sometimes talks raucously and is left at liberty to strut around the kitchen. The kitchen is its kingdom. It has a cold eye. It cocks its head and stares at me fixedly. I am very afraid and scream when it comes near. And the parrot knows. It ruffles its feathers, puffs out its chest and waddles towards me, all the while proffering the most vile curses in a hoarse voice. The bird is called Billy and was given as a present to my parents by Uncle Willy Campbell, who'd won it as a prize in some competition on board a passenger steamer between Australia and South Africa. Why do I seem to remember that my parents gave me away to Aunt Tina and Uncle Willy when I was very small? Was I to replace the child they have lost, called Breyten?

Bruinman, my eldest brother, I remember well: a robust boy fond of playing games with wooden rifles and sticks for swordfighting. Perhaps it was to be expected that he would opt for a military career. Fighting for what? For whom? Fighting for Nomansland on all the faraway frontiers from the Tugela to Timbuctoo, and many times being wounded for his pains. Phantom columns of communists will pour like a flood from the hostile underground.

Men often come up to me to talk about their adventures while serving under older brother Bruinman. They smelled Death's fetid breath on their faces. They speak of this journey with a sense of awe and of dedication to the hero. Only recently two ex-soldiers approached me on a podium where I'd made a speech. They'd been in the wars with Bruinman, one of them said. The borders drenched in blood. Ah, the Cubans they killed! And the lost comrades, the crippled and the blinded. Always knew about my being in prison, the opponent in a way, I am in their heads, but never spoken about. And now, can it not be said there was not all that much difference between your and Bruinman's combat? While Mouthpiece conveys all this, Companion scalps me with eyes like blunt bayonets, finding me a poor substitute for my brother. There are hypotheses and hippopotami better left dead in the head. Mouthpiece adds that they're lucky to be alive. Where Bruinman leads there is no turning back. And not many return. Some have their memories burnt away. Maybe they don't come back either.

Kwaaiman leaves the most vivid impression on my mind. How talented he is, strumming the guitar in a school band from a very young age, making music at home with Mother playing the harmonium and Father on the second string instrument! How gentle and good with animals! He can tame anything. Always there will be at least two dogs pawing at his feet and in the yard outside he keeps a kaleidoscope of birds—some he must have nursed back to life, they are that attached to him. How he even laughs with brown children!

BABSIE VAN ZYI

In the museum I ask for the portrait which was here on this wall only recently, and now nobody remembers ever having seen it. If it weren't for Lotus, my only true memory, who knows exacity where the frame was hung, I'd imagine it must have been a strange dream.

Old Mrs. Keet? Wasn't she the midwife long before any of us were born? The curator has blue eyes made bigger and more innocent by her glasses. Yes, she thinks there may be something in the archives. You're certainly most welcome to look.

The museum has made an effort, with the help of Kobus Kriel of Pietersfontein, to collate all available information on the medicinal plants and the herbs so richly indigenous to these parts. The remedies were passed down by Khoi and San (Hottentot and Bushman) and pioneer Boer families to their coloured descendants who now work on the farms in the district.

In the veld the sun is a lazy hand on the skin. But here the women wear kerchiefs around their hair, their brown faces are creased with laughter. They work in a room at the back to sort heaps of aromatic leaves and sticks from plants collected and cultivated by the museum, and make up little paper bags of prescriptions for all imaginable ailments.

In the converted church with its exhibits as the living souvenirs of death, an elderly brown lady sells the parcels over the counter to the rare visitors. The names of the plants already constitute a dictionary of experience. On the tongue one can taste and trace the merging of purpose and description.

Aambeibos or *Meidjiejanwillemse* (wild gentian) is used for piles. *Balderjan* for sleeplessness and constipation. *Bloublomsalie* (wild sage) for influenza, chest complaints, headaches, burns, stomachache. *Buchu* for bruises, kidneys, bladder, gout, rheumatism. *Dawidjies* for snake bite, abscess, weak stomach. *Geneesbossie* for sores on hands. *Slanghoutjie* or snake root for boils, croup, enlarged glands. Pomegranate peel as a laxative. *Harpuisbos* (resin bush) against burns and thorns. *Hondebossie* for cramps, convulsions, eczema. Hottentot bedding for heart trouble, nerves, backache. Hottentot fig for mouth sores and St. Anthony's fire. Cancer bush for cancer. Blessed thistle for gall and diphtheria. Castor-oil plant leaves for wounds and pimples. Small mallow for sore throat and carbuncles. Wild hemp for high blood pressure. *Kraalbos* for the prostate gland. Touch-me-not for rheumatic fever. Lye bush for vomiting. *Misbredie* (pigweed) for corns, asthma, acid stomach in babies, palpitations. Milkweed for distemper in dogs. *Plakkie* for festering ears. Pipestem bush for women's ailments. *Stinkkruid* for convulsions caused by worms. *Muishondbos* for high blood pressure. Thyme for tetanus, nervous disorders, flatulence. Prickly-pear leaf for arthritis and rheumatism of the hands. Arum-lily leaf for inflamed chest. Wild garlic for malaria. Violet leaves for bronchitis. Mistletoe for dropsy. *Wilde-als* for sweaty feet. Wild *dagga* for catarrh, stroke, cancer of the stomach, jaundice, poisoning . . .

And more concoctions and mixtures for bed-wetting, anemia, poor circulation, cholesterol, emphysema, heart defects, whooping cough, liver ailments, loose stomach, ulcer, menopause, migraine, water retention, sinus, goiter, indigestion, stress, spastic colon, diabetes, hardening of the arteries . . .

While Lotus and I sniff at the array of parcelled miracle cures, the elderly brown lady is watching us attentively without letting on. You don't want any remedies? Did *meneer* say *meneer* is interested in old Mrs. Keet?

No, she remembers. Many years ago Babsie van Zyl put together a file. Did *meneer* ever meet Babsie van Zyl? No? A strange woman. Difficult to know. She came from a well-off family, there was a rich farm in the district, and here she lived all by herself in a big house without a bathroom, never bothered with comforts. She is long since dead now, the ways of the world are mysterious and dark.

Does *meneer* know François Krige? Yes, I do know François Krige the painter, brother of Uys Krige the poet, who lies obliterated by the sun in his grave in the dunes, covered by a glitter of periwinkle shells. Well, Babsie was very friendly with François and his wife Sylvia. That's a Krige painting on the wall over there, the dark one of the Karoo funeral. The oils glisten like freshly turned soil.

She never married, Babsie. But was she attractive! *Meneer* should have seen her. Smoked cigarettes and curled her hair and in the evening she danced all by herself on the dark stoep to the sound of gramophone records. She had a pet monkey who screeched and jumped up and down when the music stopped. Some say there was a man who went off to war and never returned. With a moustache and oiled hair and sleeves rolled up high above the elbows so that you could see where the brown skin became white. Who knows? We all had a man who went to war. And in the old days many men had moustaches, but a tame monkey is not a common sight in Montagu. Babsie did so much for the museum and the community. *Ja, meneer* . . .

She knows everything we have in this museum from front to back. How Babsie got to be so interested in Mrs. Keet, I can't rightly tell you, *meneer*. What I do know is that she went to interview all the old people still alive about the midwife.

Why? She was funny after the man doesn't come back from the war. She put together her files in the back room where we keep the stock. The material must still all be in there somewhere.

A ROOM OF FORGETTING

The next few weeks I spend delving into the archives. One walks through the large room of chattering women adjacent to the museum, saying Good morning, Good morning, then for a short distance through the white heat outside to a separate building, big space, light filtered through panes dusts the shelves.

Everything that can now no longer be shown is kept in here. A jumble of rejected memories. *Christ from the Cross* after Rubens, a needlework tapestry as life task of Mrs. J. H. Hofmeyr, wife of 'Onze Jan', the founder of the Afrikanerbond. A hollow bronze bust, glasses and all, of D. F. Malan, at one time the dominie of the local congregation, then the first National Party prime minister in 1948. With him came to power the morose clowns of racial superiority who would eventually take us down the road to a future where the earth was stuffed with tortured corpses. Nobody wants to know him anymore. Also the clean and very neat skull of a Bushman, no teeth, a bullet hole in the forehead. On the skull is written: *Koos Sas.* Shelves of fluff and boxes of dust. A tomb marker of wood the shape of a surfboard, a chiselled text in capital letters, remembering Christina Johanna van Zyl, née Jordaan, who died on 14 January 1864 at the age of 81 years and 6 months: *"For thou shalt die and not live."*

This 'room of forgetting' behind the museum is a place of oblivion and obnubilation. Underneath cracked glass one may observe photographed bodies stiffly encased in formal clothes, the faces with keen eyes dying to be remembered. A series of children's books remind me of my first reading experiences. These stories of *'Jakkals en Wolf'* (Fox and Wolf), or a whole tribe of knowing and impudent baboons, were written and drawn by a local resident now long since gone up the mountain to higher understanding. Who will ever read them again? I remember the songs sung by Chris Blignaut with his banjo voice and broad, mocking laughter. Often animal fables, now and then with a sly dig at the authorities of the day. The Boere always struggling to move beyond the reach of the Company, the government, the British, the State. After every lost liberation war they narrow their eyes and look at the horizon, they take refuge in trees, they go off into the hills or the desert, behind the mirages, to the high plateaux where the world is black and glassy. They talk to the animals, they learn from them. It would be more correct to say they imbibe a familiarity with animal lore from the other, older indigenous people.

In one corner there are stone-age implements originating from the 'guano caves' on Derdeheuwel, the Kriel farm. Old Mr. Charlie Ravenscroft, a wagon maker who arrived from Swellendam in 1860, keen hunter and fisherman, discovered the caves while following a small buck. He saw that the caves were full of bat manure accumulated over the ages. Also implements left by generations of San nomads. Some of these tools and weapons he sent to the museum of natural history in Cape Town.

In the 1870s and '80s there is no nearby market for the farmers' produce. That is why they sell bat dung. They also dry their fruit and take wagon-loads full all the way up to the diamond fields around Kimberley. Money has to be borrowed for these long, hazardous trips. The lenders are a bank at Swellendam and the Dutch Reformed Church at Montagu. When interest on the loan is due, only too painfully often, the farmer sends a brown workman on foot to Swellendam. These messengers cover the distance in an incredibly short time by routes that have now been forgotten. But it is true that the small sinewy men have an inbred knowledge of the drift of clouds and the lay of mountains. They walk with the wind.

"Many people from Montagu left on the 1870 diamond rush to Pniel and Du Toitspan outside present-day Kimberley. Clothing was practically unobtainable there. Van Zyl once saw a man exchange a horse (or an ox) for a panama hat. Whenever anyone found a diamond they used to shout a certain word (I forget what) and everybody dropped whatever they were doing and dashed to the scene. Once a particularly loud ballyhoo brought hundreds of people to the scene of a dog fight. People were panting with heat, dust, excitement. Van Zyl brought back one diamond—on a ring on his wife's finger. There was a fund for mutual assistance created by the Montagu miners, but the proceeds went to the Dutch Reformed Church." (This from a document I find in a shoe box on a shelf in the room of obliterated memories, probably left there by Babsie van Zyl; the Van Zyl in the text may have been an ancestor.)

Just below the bat caves a Kriel forebear discovers a source of water. (The San know what happens in the earth, they trace the veins, they walk under the ground to go visit the rain bull.) Kriel and his labourers construct a furrow from this source, cracking the rocks by alternate fires and cold water. They cannot afford dynamite. Then they painstakingly knead clay in ox hides to plaster the furrow because cement also is too expensive. The furrows thus bitten out of the hard rockface are still in use.

It is 1880 and old Mr. Charlie Ravenscroft has made a little money speculating with bat droppings and sun-dried apricots. He buys dynamite to go fishing in the Breërivier. Look, there he is in his small boat in the middle of the stream, the reflection bobbing on the surface. He lights a stick and it explodes before he can throw it. Oh look, his hand is mangled as if eaten by a *boerboel*, the water is red! He shouts with fear and pain. A brown worker, sitting patiently among the reeds in the vicinity, singing softly to himself, not bothering anybody, hears him, plunges into the water to bring the skiff to the riverbank, runs like the wind to Robertson to fetch the doctor. The hand is amputated, the stump later fitted with a hook. The hook can still be seen in the back room, its curled shape in memory of the functions of a hand.

RACHEL SUSANNA KEET

The documents pertaining to my great-grandmother consist of a number of lined double-page folios. The handwriting in blue ink is large and easy on the eye. The photos referred to in the text are no longer in the file. On the last page there's a sketched map indicating where Mrs. Keet's house stood. That too is now gone. Then a firm signature—*Babsie van Zyl*—and a date, 26/8/1966.

The people interviewed by Babsie van Zyl (dozens, she says) are ancient and flat like the newspapers of another time, their words are like dead mosquitoes. They have to send back their memories a long way. Mist flows up the mountains. We cannot know what they talk about. They contradict one another. They don't speculate. Perhaps they only leave some things unsaid. For instance, in the following extracts from some of the declarations there are references to a man living with Ouma Keet. Her offspring? An adopted child? A lover? Sometimes he is old; then young. Then there is the question of the black boy, Klaas, who dies or who does not die.

Reading about my great-grandmother is like listening to someone else describing the dusty light coming through the windows of a room where dead memories are kept.

***Mr. Gert Swart (over 80) c/o Mrs. Justice Hill, corner of Barry and Long Streets** As a young man in the early*

1900s he boarded with Mrs. Keet for years (while he was working in Montagu and before he started farming). Also boarding with her was Dawid Reynecke, who was an elderly bachelor and who originally came from the Orange Free State.

According to Mr. Swart, Mrs. Keet was a handsome woman of an exceptionally cheerful and amusing disposition and a kind and generous nature. She was considered very good in her work...

He doesn't know anything about her husband and has always assumed that she was a widow. Knows nothing about her family background, but remembers one daughter—a Mrs. Martha Wentzel—who lived at Bonnievale. She has since died and a daughter of hers (he's forgotten her name) still lives at the Strand. This daughter happened to be staying with her when she suddenly died of a stroke on the 16th or 17th of May, 1915. He thinks she was then a woman of about seventy-odd.

Why he remembers it so well is because his own wife Lettie had just given birth to their only child Minnie in Mrs. Keet's house. She was the last child delivered by her and she herself died a day or two after the birth. Minnie was born on 15th May 1915. (Mr. Swart had brought his wife from the farm where he was then living.)

Martha Wentzel (whose husband's name was Piet) either was a midwife at the time of her mother's death or became one soon afterwards, operating, presumably, in the Bonnievale area.

Ai Byp (corruption of 'babe' or 'baby'—old coloured servant of the Nothlings *Knew Mrs. Keet well. Says she worked quite a lot among the coloured people especially in cases of difficult births. Charged them ten shillings. Remembers Mrs. Keet assisting at the birth of her (Ai Byp's) brother*

Christiaan (pronounced "Krisjan" by all and sundry in Montagu).

She knew the coloured lad who was brought up by Mrs. Keet well. His name was Klaas and he was pitch black, she says. He lived on Mrs. Keet's premises and as a small child she used to dress him in short khaki pants, a shirt with elastic round the waist and a small white apron. When he grew up he used to drive Mrs. Keet's trap which, she says, was not a one-horse trap but was pulled by two small deep black ponies.

After Mrs. Keet's death Klaas came to live in the location. During the 1918 flu she recalls how he was one of those taken to the Mission Church in Long Street, where he died. All the seriously ill coloured people were transported to the Mission Church. Those who got better were taken to convalesce in the Mission School next door. Klaas unfortunately succumbed.

After Mrs. Keet's death a Mrs. Swanepoel took over her work in Montagu among both coloured and whites. When Mrs. Swanepoel died her work among the coloured people was taken over by Kaaitjie Pokwas and Louisa Doris (two coloured women, Louisa pronounced "Lewiesa" by the coloured people)...

Incidentally, Mrs. Nothling says that the Dawid Reyneke (who evidently was also brought up by Mrs. Keet) worked for old Mr. Frans du Toit on his farm in Long Street. (Last house on the right as you go towards the Barrydale road—still stands. The du Toits one of the first families to settle here.)

Mrs. Malie Kriel, Cypress, Montagu, Phone 1302
Knew Mrs. Keet well. Their 'tuishuis' *(house used by the farmers when they came to the village on business or to church) was directly opposite her house. They frequently had meals with Mrs. Keet. She remembers her as a very kind and hospitable woman, with a sunny and cheerful nature, rather*

witty and amusing. She frequently managed to make her pa-
tients laugh in spite of their severe pains.

In her work she appears to have been very able and clever.
Knew what to do in an emergency. Mrs. Kriel knows of one
instance where a woman's bladder came unstuck with the
birth. Old Mrs. Keet put it back and fixed it up and the
woman recovered with no ill aftereffects. She often took
women in and they were confined in her own house. In those
days money was very scarce and she charged only one pound
per confinement. Later on this was raised to one pound ten
shillings. This charge included a daily visit for eight to ten
days after the birth. She frequently worked with Dr. Muller.

Mrs. Kriel knows nothing about Mrs. Keet's husband or
children except for a young lad, Dawid Reyneke, who lived
with and was brought up by her. Mrs. Kriel thinks he was
her nephew (child of her sister). One of the last confinements
done by her was that of Mrs. Gert Swart (Lettie Hill) when
she gave birth to Minnie Swart (now Minnie Nel—mother
of Marianna Odendal, the hairdresser). This must have been
1914 or '15. She died soon afterwards. Cause of death or age
at the time was not known. She always wore a long coat with
a very long scarf when she went out to confinements.

Mrs. M. van der Merwe, du Toit Street (Phone 357)
Remembers the one-horse trap Mrs. Keet used on her con-
finements and subsequent visits. She tells of a young coloured
lad who used to drive this trap. She says this lad died very
suddenly and Mrs. Keet died shortly afterwards. I, personally,
think she is confusing him with the child, Dawid Reyneke,
mentioned by Mrs. Malie Kriel. Mrs. van der Merwe remem-
bers there was something unusual about this death. I think
old Mrs. Keet was very heartsore and it probably hastened
her own death. Mrs. van der Merwe was just a young girl
at the time and didn't take overmuch notice.

Mrs. Nothling (now 84 and bedridden) 3 Le Roux Street, Phone 314 *Recalls that in a house very near them lived a certain Koos van Zyl, whose wife, Nonnie, was a daughter of Mrs. Keet. She knows nothing about any other children, but says that Mrs. Keet and her husband did not get on and by the time Mrs. Keet settled in Montagu they were either living apart or he had already died.*

Mrs. Abri Jordaan (Scriba) *Remembers seeing Mrs. Keet standing, arms akimbo, outside the primary school watching the small children with rather a proprietory air and saying:* "Almal my bobbejane" *(All my baboons).*

Mrs. Roy Euvrard, du Toit Street (Phone 162) *Remembers seeing her often as a child, but when she came to settle here after her marriage to Mr. George Barry in 1914 she seems to think old Mrs. Keet was already dead. Old Mrs. Keet one day said to her: "My child, you must never take up my profession."*

Mrs. Euvrard added that child mortality in those days was rather high in Montagu and contrary to what Mrs. Malie Kriel told me, says old Mrs. Keet was rather slapdash in her methods. But then child mortality was high everywhere and I'm inclined to believe Mrs. Kriel, as she had personal experience of Mrs. Keet, who delivered five of her children.

Mrs. Jaap le Roux, Piet Retief Street (near football field) *She is eighty-eight and bedridden but mental faculties OK. Mother of Mrs. Sannie Kriel (Sannie Saadjie, "Little Seed"). She had thirteen children, any number of which were brought into the world by Mrs. Keet. The last one where Mrs. K assisted was born in 1913. Sannie Saadjie herself went to call Mrs. Keet as her father (Oom Jaap) was away from home. He was a* transportryer *(transport driver). Mrs. le*

Roux says her next child was delivered by a Mrs. Stemmet and she therefore presumes that Mrs. Keet must have died between 1913 and 1915 as she would not have employed someone else if Mrs. Keet had been alive.

Mrs. Comie Kriel, corner of Kohler and Joubert Streets (just below Mrs. Epsie) *She was a Miss Rossouw from Laatsrivier, Koo. She says she remembers that her parents bought the sweet little white enamel bath (used by Mrs. Keet to bathe the babies) on the sale after Mrs. Keet's death. It was much used on the farm before they moved into the village in 1927. She cannot remember precisely when that sale took place. Her husband (Mr. Gideon Kriel) remembers fetching Mrs. Keet to the confinement of his mother at the birth of his youngest brother in 1912.*

Issie Adler, Piet Retief Street (Phone 181) (Mr. Georg Brink's sister) *Issie tells me the following gruesome story about Mrs. Keet. It was told her by her mother and she assures me it's true although she says nobody else will tell me this tale if they happen to know about it.*

According to her a man (she thinks he was called Walker) came to fetch Mrs. Keet to his wife's confinement in the middle of the night and when they got to the house, he tackled her on the stoep and raped her, whereupon Mrs. Keet, when it was all over, calmly took up her bag, went into the house and delivered the poor woman!

MOTHER/FAMILY

My mother and her sisters and brothers—they were thirteen in all—were of an exceptionally cheerful disposition. When they met, which was often, there were endless stories and jokes laced with laughter. They would slap their thighs and bend double as if shouting at the earth. They would quote to one another the many funny sayings of their mother (my *ouma*, Rachel Susanna Cloete), who died before my birth. This grandmother was still young when she went over to the other side of memory, probably exhausted from giving birth to so many people, and it became my mother's task to bring up the younger siblings.

In family albums there are snapshots of young women with bobbed hair and short white dresses tighter around the knees than the waist, dancing what looks like the Charleston on the grass in front of a farmhouse. In other scenes they wear brimless hats fitting close to the head and low over the brow.

I have difficulty imagining them young: the smooth limbs of my mother, her honey hair; the tight belly of my father, his back and his buttocks, his chin and his klipspringer eyes. I want to bring these youngsters under a protective wing and warn them about the shards of broken bottles lying ahead, how you will cut your hands when you open the earth, the dismantling of the body, the opacity of eyesight, the dark ink of memory staining the pages so that the mornings become illegible. Can these be the same people whom I live with in later life and who are now whispers under a cement slab on a hillside near the ocean?

Nearly all of my mother's family speak with funny voices coming through the nose. They often have to clear their throats. I see her shaken by fits of red-faced coughing as if attempting to dislodge a swallowed morsel from the windpipe. She bends double. Aunt Susan dies from cancer of the vocal cords. All of them have fine hearing: they pick up and carry a tune in church and at Whitsun prayer meetings, or when on a picnic outing. Aunt Anna, treading the dispossessed harmonium, still sings from somewhere between nose and throat with a sure, angelic voice. Keeping in practice to join the choir of brothers and sisters jiving on the lawn up there before the pearly gates.

In the Cloete family we have a history of weak lungs. I myself choked to death at the age of seven, and ever since I periodically get blue in the face. Comes the first splattering of winter raindrops and a fog descends on Kwaaiman's chest; day and night he wears a knitted cap pulled down over the ears, he says *ja-ja*, such is life, and sips warmed alcohol to ward off the sniffles and a hoarse voice. In his younger years when his hair was the colour of honey, he briefly had one lung blighted by tuberculosis.

In fact, I have little verifiable information about my ancestors. I know about the first Cloete, Jacob (considered a Jacobin), who was the original owner of Constantia, South Africa's most prestigious wine estate. There is an expression in Afrikaans about Vader Jacob at night making the rounds with a lantern to see if all the doors are securely locked. He was killed on 23 May 1693 by runaway soldiers probably trying to get at his wine. Produce from this farm was the regular tipple of Bonaparte in exile on St. Helena, much appreciated with a smacking of lips. Baudelaire refers in a poem to *"le vin de Constance."* I also know that the name Cloete comes from Kluthe, Kloete or Kloot, which in turn derives from Chludio and Chlodowig. The family coat of arms shows a falconer with falcon, and the words *Ubi cras.*

The tribe increased wondrously. Very early on there was a bifurcation when one Gerrit Cloete set out to create his own. He would make Afrikaners, the first meaning of the word indicating a descendant of the mixing of 'European' and 'African'. His second and third marriages were to 'non-white' women. Catherina, a daughter from his first, 'white,' wife, taking a leaf from her father's vigorous book, had several children by Klaas Barends: *"Bêrent, een regte Hottentot"* (a genuine Hottentot). The offspring spread through Namakwaland, the Richtersveld, Suid-Wes—present-day Namibia. Family names recur frequently: Sebastiaan, Hendrik, Kaaitjie van die Kaap (Cape Cathy). My mother's name was Catherina Johanna, the family called her *Kaaitjie* or *Kitty* (but her name may also bear the trace of one Rynier Frederik Marthinus Keet, passed away in 1894, who had as second spouse Catherina Johanna Rossouw); my youngest brother, Hartman, was christened Sebastiaan after a maternal uncle and an older cousin; my grandfather was Oupa Hendrik.

This brown part of our family increased dramatically when slavery was abolished. Some Cloetes were the wealthy owners of a large human stock. The freed slaves inherited or took for themselves the clan's name. Henceforth there were considerably more 'brown' Cloetes than 'white' ones in the country.

Some descendants became integrated with the English. They waxed their moustaches and went into politics. Sir Abraham Josias Cloete (Kokstad 7/8/1794– London 26/10/1886) became a professional dog of war. He was sent to occupy Tristan da Cunha in order to foil Napoleon's attempt at escaping from captivity on St. Helena. In 1823 he fought a duel on the back porch of a stately Cape mansion with Dr. James Barry, the physician attached to the person of Governor Lord Charles Somerset. The flashing of blades was caused by a deprecating remark made by Barry about Christina Sara

Dreyer, who was destined for wedlock with Abraham's younger brother, Johan Gerhard Cloete.

In 1842 Sir Abraham commanded the detachment of British soldiers dispatched to relieve Port Natal (Durban) which was under siege from Voortrekkers. Swirling battles were fought for possession of that outpost on the tropical coast and the fertile soil and rolling hills further inland. (Soon it would be declared a British colony.) A river ran red with the blood of Zulu warriors slain by Voortrekkers with firesticks sheltering in their circle of wagons. They prayed their god down from the clouds and ensured his services by a covenant of promises. One Afrikaner general wears a top hat and his arm, wounded by a Zulu spear, in a sling. His cheeks are clean-shaven, his waistcoat embroidered.

Sir Abraham's brother, the lawyer Hendrik (Henry) Cloete (15/6/1792–26/12/1870), was appointed Commissioner of Natal in 1843. In 1854 he too was elevated to knighthood. Sir Henry participated in all the border wars. His sword was red. This has always been a violent country. In 1856 he was a major general in charge of military forces on the Windward and Leeward Islands in the West Indies. He bedded and married the governor's daughter. In 1871 he was promoted to general and became known as "the father of the British Army."

There must be a heart beating under the bemedalled tunic. Already in 1847 he peers into the future, worries about the land of his birth, he looks high and he looks low and writes an article in the *Edinburgh Review* entitled "What is to be done with our criminals?" He proposed liberal measures of reform and rehabilitation and re-insertion. He was also one of the first historians of the Great Trek.

Where does our grandfather, Johannes Hendrik

Cloete, hail from? He is a gentleman down on his luck, working for the Divisional Council in the Bredasdorp district. Soft-spoken and laughing apologetically when he clears his throat, which is often, he wears a soft hat and thick-lensed glasses and a waistcoat with a watch chain. His boots are shiny and laced up to the ankles, but I have a feeling the feet inside must be vulnerable. He sired many children.

In the Montagu graveyard we find headstones for Johannes Hendrik Cloete (24/7/1881−7/10/1958)—a cousin of my grandfather? Pieter Wouter Cloete (18/3/1843−17/11/1916) and Christina J. Cloete, born De Kock, deceased at the age of 63 years and 8 months; and Jan Sebastian Cloete (8/4/1869−31/7/1927) and his wife, Hester Helena, née Burger (28/1/1871−8/6/1951)—are these perhaps my great-grandparents?

FATHER/FAMILY

The Breytenbach side is more confused. People lose all remembrance of a land of origin. Their language is phased out imperceptibly, to be replaced by a vigorous bastard tongue. Their clothes become looser, their skins darker (or lighter). They retain traces of ancient characteristics as soldiers or minstrels or nomads. But they worry about roots: it is painful to have neither before nor after. Dream merchants (the psychologists of their time) visit the villages and the farms, for a stiff price they will establish a tree of genealogy. You will be somebody.

In the twelfth century there is a family called Von Breitenbach zu Breitenfelde. A wolf's head sits depicted at the top of the heraldic shield. Among the *Glücksritter*, fortune seekers in the employ of the Dutch East India Company who established a trading post on the southern tip of the continent, there is a Coenraad Breytenbach, soldier by profession, who disappears from history into the interior. (The urge can be summed up in the dying words of an old rogue, Trader Horn alias Aloysius Smith: "Where's me bloody passport? I'm off to Africa.")

In 1737 Johann Jacob Breytenbach (from Würzburg) lands at the Cape, the big wind blows spray over the jetty, he soon becomes a *vryburger* (free citizen) and goes to farm in the district of Swellendam. The family makes its living from ostriches. One never really tames an ostrich—the only way to intimidate it is to threaten its eyes with a branch from the thorn tree. For the first few weeks the young live from the excrement of the parent birds. When roused they can outrun a horse.

A descendant, also called Johann Jacob, decides to move to the Boland with his nine sons and his ostriches. But he only gets as far as the Breërivier, where he buys a farm near Bonnievale along the shiny stretch of water. His sons have to bring the patriarch's possessions over the mountain. Two of them are on the wagon pulled by donkeys, the others will herd along the ostriches. When it is dark the birds follow a lantern or a torch. With the load are also the family's coffins. How will you be laid away if you are too poor to afford a coffin at the time of your death? Will you be thrown to the dogs?

They take turns sleeping in one of the coffins, where it is reassuring and warm. It is night when the wagon lurches over the neck of the mountain. The donkeys bray at the salt-white moon. The descent is steep, the shadows are deep, and the load shifts, crushing to death the brother sleeping in the coffin. He who holds the reins only notices at sunrise that his brother has exchanged the temporary for the eternal.

The old man rules the family with patriarchal authority. He chews tobacco and is very secure in directing the juice of the cud at the feet of the target of his displeasure. His wife is a girl Olivier. Death comes for the paterfamilias; he is put to earth on the slope of Vrotkop. It is said that his grave is marked by a stone with this inscription: *"Nooit had een klag oor zijn lippen gegaan/Al biggelt daar ook oor zijn wang een traan."* (Never a complaint escaped his lips, even if a tear coursed down his cheek.)

My Oupa Jan must be one of the eight surviving sons. How did he become so poor? Did his ostriches run away? It is known that relations between sons and father, and between brothers, were strained. Although they continued living in the same region, the family contacts are buried in silence. After Oupa Jan Bruinman loses his first wife to the snake, he marries a widow surnamed Olivier. Ouma Annie's high cheekbones and flattish nose remind one that many people see a relationship between Asian and Khoisan people. Does her husband sit in the branches to keep an eye out for his brothers? When you see a Breytenbach coming, shout at the top of your voice to chase him away. Dead ostriches come tumbling down with the flood, their wings like entangled sails.

I'm still small when I spend time with Oupa Jan and Ouma Annie in Bonnievale. Grandfather never goes to church, but he's a religious man nevertheless. I offer to take the Holy Book with his mug of morning coffee out to him, I know he likes to keep it close at hand. Ouma Annie says I must stop playing under the pepper tree and leave him at peace up there. It is closer to heaven.

Children should be seen and not heard. Much later I overhear an uncle explaining softly to a circle of men with red faces and puffed cheeks how Oupa Jan rolls his strong tobacco as cigarettes in the pages of the family Bible, to modify Scripture by inhaling the Truth of our Saviour. He says the names of the family written on the flyleaf will go up in smoke, and with it our memory. The men often look over their shoulders. One day he will set fire to himself, the uncle says. Who's going to believe us? People will say we've killed an angel or hanged a communist!

There is an elderly woman living with my grandparents—they give her shelter and she looks after them. I know somehow she must be an impoverished relative from my mother's side, although I don't know the nature of the family bond. Later I realise she must be a spinster or a widow. Her grey hair is pinned back in a bun and she always wears an apron. She has long, yellowish buck teeth. She often laughs through her nose and then scrapes her throat with a cough. I remember her as Aunt Grieta Wentzel.

Later still I'm told she assisted my mother when I was born. Her hands are wet and red, she must be wearing the apron to hide them.

There's a photo of me and my grandfather, I'm about seven years old, soon I'll be dead, and I stand between his knees, his trouser legs are out of shape because of the constant squatting, they sag in *bokkniee* (goat's knees). My head is shaven, I am dressed in short khaki pants and a shirt with elastic around the waist. My mother has sewn the outfit with her own hands. I even remember Oupa Jan's smell, spicy like that of an old goat.

Now Kwaaiman comes to the house, his woollen cap

pulled over the ears. He rubs his hands and whistles to a little green-backed bird who emits a monotonous plaintive call from high up in the belhambra. Then he glances at the photo of me and Oupa Jan reproduced on the flyleaf of my 1973 book and grumbles out the side of his mouth: By the way, this photo supposedly of you and Oupa—it's not you at all, it's *me* there between his legs . . . Look high, look low. Look closer at the faded snapshot: all of a sudden I look strange to myself.

MEMORY/THE LORRY

The lorry gets this far with tremendous difficulty. Frightening rain, pouring rain, rain like sliding mountains out of the void and the mist devastate the land, shifting embankments and misspelling torrents and washing roads away. It can finally slide no further and now lies sobbed to the axles in the slurry of the last incline before reaching the farmyard. Mud is of an orange colour. When the showers abate and heavens suddenly expose a silk-blue underlayer, I see angels walking hither and thither up there. They too are soaked to the skin. The only solution is to carry Greatfather piggyback as far as the homestead. Like an ancient praying mantis (the god of the Hottentots), stiff as a stick with rheumatism, he climbs from the back of the lorry where he sat so wet and miserable onto my shoulders. He is making little puffing and sucking sounds with the lips, maybe to count a mouthful of old words. His goatee, shivered to greyness, gleams in the wind, and the wrinkles over his cheekbones are puckered. For an old Chinaman like him life is one long journey of steps into nothingness, with Greatmother as destination, that ancient woman with milk in the eyes, lying in the four-poster in the old house's darkened bedroom. I totter with Greatfather on my shoulders, *schlug-schlug* through the mush, as far as the back door to the kitchen. The dog then and there barks an inapplicable page from the dictionary. This is no time for erudition; dying is not a text. In the kitchen, around a table, three very old servants are seated with veils over their faces—presumably to keep the flies away from the dark milk. They're playing cards. Before them they have glasses deep with ruby-red wine, from which the light is drinking. A glass without wine has no inner sound. Greatfather's lips warble as if he intends to conjure a flock of mouth-moistenened birds from the unseen. With this insignificant bundle of old man's flesh on my shoulders I shuffle towards the bedroom, and then it strikes me that I've forgotten to greet the three loyal bodies, dark now as flies in the winter, and so long confined by rain to the kitchen. Awkwardly I bend down to lift the corner of a veil and to buss a sombre, tart, crumpled cheek, and say: Ah, good people, please excuse me. You girls are so young and so pretty and so *bushy-tailed* that I didn't recognise you at all.

MEMORY

When my parents leave Bonnievale it is to move to a farm near Riversdal. We cross deserts and the sky is leprous with stars. We have to stop often so that I may vomit my heart out by the side of the road. My mother is unhappy, she doesn't laugh as often. My father's face is black. At the time of shimmering heat over the fields a couple of very ancient nomads come trudging out of the distance. The past is a distant place. The past makes things from far away suddenly appear near to one, like a mirage. Because of the shivering light they seem to float without feet. Pai and Mai are their names, so they say softly, their skins are so distended and full of loose folds you'd think they're wrapped in finely tanned animal hides. They build a hut of sticks and reeds on the farm, round like a hat without a brim. They sit on their haunches in the sun before the hut, both smoking short-stemmed pipes. Mother somehow acquires a small, painted trap and a pony with a long mane. When the setting sun paints sky and mountains in the Indian colours of dying she harnesses the pony, she takes along Hartman and baby Rachel and me, we go clip-clopping towards the distance along farm roads in the gathering dusk, a wispy sigh of smoke flutters above Pai and Mai's earth-coloured hut, wind blows through our mother's hair and brings tears to her cheeks, the road never stops and night never comes.

KRISJAN

François Krige repeatedly painted Krisjan, Ai Byp's brother. The dark, gleaming canvases imbue the sitter with a melancholy glory. In this small village oasis Krisjan is painted as the emblem of a broken humanity. The folds in his face are pages blackened by history, marked in a foreign tongue. Krisjan is King Lear. His majesty and his massive presence fill the cloth. Krisjan is a deposed ruler seen through the eyes of Rembrandt. He comes from a long way away down the ages. Then François Krige painted Krisjan as Montagu knows him: a hang-about, bum, drifter, beggar, sleeping wherever

the alcohol closes in upon him in rain or in sun, a sad nomad with filthy rags twisted around his head, an oversized and shapeless and torn overcoat, all his belongings in the one bag slung across his shoulder. In the past the old people trekked through the mountains with all their belongings across their shoulders in bags made of soft skin.

WIND TONGUE

Through the ages people leave only the flutter of a shadow behind, a whisper in the leaves on branches. It is the wind talking to itself. Some old men climb into the trees to learn the language of whispering.

This museum is housed in what used to be the Long Street Mission Church. People came to die in great numbers within its walls during the influenza epidemic when it was converted into a house of passing away, of dark wind. It is believed that the epidemic—some refer to it as the Spanish Plague—began with the gathering of a crowd to rejoice at the Armistice of 1918. Peace festivities propagated the killer disease. The old Salvation Army hall became a makeshift hospital for whites. A soup kitchen for coloured people was opened in the Ebenezer Church hall. All three local doctors fell ill (Wessels, Muller, and Mrs. Müller). Reverend van Huyssteen, minister to the Dutch Reformed congregation, admonished the voluntary workers to eat a little salt, take some snuff, and tie small bags of garlic and *wilde-als* around their waists. Maybe it helped. In any event, the death rate was not as high as, for example, in Touwsrivier across the mountains. There one particularly sombre moment of mass dying was known as 'The Black Night'.

But nothing could save pregnant women. All those who fell ill would be blown up the mountain. Their infants were already dead in the lap, the placenta a shroud and the umbilical cord a stem of black congealed blood.

Church services were conducted in the open air, under the tall trees of Lovers Walk. People were afraid to whisper to one another. Would you stop breathing on me! When wind rustled through the branches they looked up and put a finger to their lips. Then they saw an old scout perched high and motioned to him to hush the soft passing footfalls, please. (*Let us have a minute of silence here, you tongues of Satan!*)

Burial proceedings were not held in the churches either; there were short and simple graveside ceremonies with mourners gathered at a safe distance on the outskirts of the graveyard, cloths fastened over their noses and mouths. No shortage of coffins and no lack of gravediggers would however be reported.

When *trekboere* (migrant farmers) a century or two earlier 'discovered' the river steaming from the earth's bowels and followed its course into the narrow gap between mountains of petrified flame, they must have believed they'd found a source of miracle water outside Christian theology. One of them severely hurt his hand when trying to dislodge a wagon wheel stuck between rocks; for days he bathed the wound in the strange-tasting liquid, and he soon saw that it had healing qualities. Nature is bountiful. The people who lived here tell us their god can be a tortoise or a mantis or a trickster called Kaggen.

The church followed the settler pioneers. You might say it refused to let them out of its sight. Already in

1854 a congregation was formed with Servaas Hofmeyr as the first shepherd of the flock. Dr. Joseph Castles became the resident doctor. He would try and save hands bitten off by dogs, but needed the help of a midwife to snip babies free from their mothers' wombs. In 1855 Bernardus Keet was the teacher. Might he be related to the great-grandfather about whom nobody knows anything?

At the entrance to the kloof where this warm water emerges, a house with a steep roof of shiny corrugated iron was built by Mr. Eyssen. Enormous mountain tortoises and peacocks came to live around the dwelling.

At the other end of the canyon, on the property of Uitvlucht, the Montagu Baths would be built. Successive owners were New Cape Central Railways; Jannie Marais; Fernandes of Madeira, who had the hotel painted in bright colours; Hugh Trevis, a millionnaire from Australia who brought along a white parrot; Aaron Idelson, a hotel keeper from town; and ultimately the municipality. They added a trailer park and a public swimming pool. There was much music and drunkenness and gambling. Easy money changes hands.

The church could not see around the mountain and could not hear the wind talking. When the Great Flood came it was a Sunday and everything was swept away. In Bath Kloof all the trees were uprooted, the Eyssen house was engulfed, the trees of Lovers Walk snapped like matchsticks. The old men who saw it unfurling remained paralysed in their nests and died with a jubilant song on their lips.

It would all be rebuilt. Now, at night, middle-aged white roosters with sagging bellies come from Cape Town. In the steaming hot pools lithe brown girls with gaps where their front teeth used to be exhibit their smooth bodies. They make sibilant sounds like birds. The bald cocks ogle and dream dreams and slurp their whiskies. They try to pull in the flab. In due time couples repair to rooms in the hotel.

Eagles nest high among the crags. Halfway up the mountain face is a cave where 'Bushmen' lived for centuries. The approaches, the entrance and the walls inside are now entirely covered by graffiti, mostly initials, like layer upon layer of mindless excreta.

FRANÇOIS KRIGE

I first learned of François Krige when I was still at school, through the book of his brother Uys, *Sol y Sombra*, for which he'd made companion drawings. An illuminating title for them both: the play, the texture of light and darkness, the way the drawings capture more than the scenes depicted, gently but insistently drawing you in, making you participate; and in this procedure, as I realised only much later, he was showing total generosity, as he would all through his life. He was *sharing*. Later still, I would come to understand his wisdom in giving only enough for the receiver (or the guest) to become autonomous—because the greater generosity is in neither pretending to give more than you have nor giving more than the recipient can take.

But not for nothing is the book called *Sun and Shadow*; the reference is also to bullfighting, that deathly art of dappled clarity and surging obscurity, where the seats are priced according to whether you sit in the *sombra* or in the *sol*, when you watch the sword of sunlight piercing and releasing the flood of nightfall.

François Krige is very ill and it is time to go say

goodbye, I don't know whether I'll ever see him again. He is dying from cancer. As he gets closer to where the wind blows from, the doses of morphine will be increased, but not yet.

It is summer in a country of burning. With the assistance of a half-crippled old man with faraway eyes and a broad-brimmed hat, Sylvia keeps the garden alive. There are splotches of shade and splashes of colour, exactly like any of the many paintings François has made of this enclosed place of peace. The pergola is heavy with grapes. This year the artist will not pick the ripe bunches. Neither will he rest from his labours in the shadow of the back stoep, half-reclining on the divan there, to listen and to look at the many fluttering birds visiting the garden.

What can I say to him? Should I quote Hannah Arendt? "I said to myself: if it is possible to do so decently, I would really like, still, to stay in this world." Or Bian Tong? "It is better to live today than to die tomorrow." Or John XXIII, on his deathbed? "Every day is a good day to be born, every day is a good day to die."

No, he knows all there is to know. The mind can see distance coming closer. No need to waste his time with your silly jokes, your flippant prattling.

Now he is already lying in the old bed in the front bedroom with Death right next to him. Like an ancient dog with a bad smell, Death takes up more space by the day. François must be careful not to get pushed out of bed—in his frail condition he'd hurt himself on the floor. When trucks come rumbling down the road the windowpanes shudder. The well-smoked pipe with the charred bowl is within reach on a little table.

The painter has always had the appearance of a Renaissance youth. The cheeks are red, the neatly trimmed beard and hair swept back from the broad forehead are still of a golden colour despite his years. It is only when he shifts the body to find a more comfortable position that you see in how much pain he must be. Then he unconsciously starts twisting a lock of hair in his fingers, as if he were again a fearful and uncertain child.

He talks colour. We speak about Matisse—isn't it wonderful how he combined simplicity of line and vibrancy of colour fields? He reminisces about the light of cathedrals. One hasn't visited the old masters often enough. There's a sea that he still wants to explore with his eyes, some paintings which need to be made as an echo to waves on the rocks (he has a specific place in mind). He has ample spiritual power with which to paint, it is only the body which is temporarily a little tardy. One should just be patient, that's all.

He says (is he quoting?): Intelligent behaviour can only occur if the individual has developed the power not to respond immediately to stimuli. Creative innovation must partly depend upon prolonging the interval between stimulus and response.

One must be humble. We can never equal the masters. The Rembrandts I saw! And yet we must work within our time. (He has no time to waste on the superficial heat of present-day arguments about art in South Africa, all that politically correct, alienated drivel!) Yet (he smiles), as Duchamp said: "The dead should not be permitted to be so much stronger than the living."

He doesn't want to neglect his work. One must be vigilant, if you don't touch them for a while they become clotted. He very much needs to get to the studio next door to choose which works must be kept and which ones are better gotten rid of. Can that which has been imagined ever fade away totally?

He lights a cigarette. The pipe is too much of a bother. Against the walls his glowing paintings. This country will not acknowledge him, and with love and mercy he brought it to tenderness and to fire on the canvas. His hand has made so many movements, has travelled the extra mile over unexplored spaces. The hand may be knobbly now, uncertain in striking the match, but the whole being is as invisible and *right* as a Bushman's arrow, and the blue, intelligent eyes mirror something which others have not yet seen.   I think to myself: Is izt just as well he's too weak to destroy his own work. I talk to him about Kafka's instructions to Max Brod. He answers quietly. Maybe he wants to say: Go on, talk—you don't know what you're saying. What is quality? Who but the person confronting his own work ever will ever know? Is it not ultimately about the dignity of leaving a few marks?

His fingers are playing with his hair again.

He asks after Jan Rabie and Daantjie Saayman, the writer and the publisher, two old friends of ours when we were young and brave in the Cape. Has heard it said that they're not well. He should call them on the telephone. One doesn't know what to say to a sick person. Is it serious? It is as if he fully expects them to go long before he does . . .

A few weeks later we hear the news. I am told that he died in great pain, the last days and nights were not easy, he didn't sleep (before the final sleep), even large helpings of morphine brought no relief. When he was young he spent long periods in the desert, painting and drawing the Bushmen, but with the passing years, or maybe due to inattention at the last moment, because of a momentary lapse, one forgets how to die.

When he is dead the colours fade and for a while the birds do not return to the garden. Not even the owl which sometimes hooted on the roof. It is as if they know. During the previous weeks ordinary folk—brown ladies with headcloths and their hands clasped under their aprons, brown gentlemen in blue overalls turning their hats awkwardly with rough fingers—come regularly to ask after the health of *meneer* François. Sylvia looks at them with her green eyes, she greets them solemnly, she informs them exactly of the situation.

Now that it is over there's silence in and around the house. Suzanne stayed with her brother and her sister-in-law till the end. In the last days she walked with her brother through their shared youth, opening drawers and doors, greeting a gallery of long-dead ancestors, taking leave. Revel, Suzanne's husband, comes from Cape Town. In the studio, stacks of paintings and reams of drawings which nobody has ever seen are discovered. The master has left the premises, the works have been liberated from his critical eye and hand. They are now autonomous. Revel draws up plans for converting the studio house into a gallery. Attie Jass, Montagu's master builder, proudly brings roominess and light to the interior. The artworks transform the walls. On an easel the last unfinished self-portrait is exhibited, questioning eyes set in a lined face against the background of a Tibetan cloth with many Buddhas.

It was often said that François was a retiring person, discreet and unostentatious. Indeed, he shunned the public role or posture ... But, looking at what he left behind, it is evident that the work grew from an intimate interaction with his environment. He divested himself of the frills and the blasphemy of mundane salon agitation, he pared his existence down to the essential living discipline of painting and drawing, but he was no hermit. He loved his wine, his pipe, his music, his tennis, his garden, his painting expeditions, his extended overseas trips for a good hard look at the work of his predecessors, and he loved the company he kept.

I wish to make the debatable statement that François Krige—despite a certain timelessness and universality—worked in Afrikaans, in terms of both subject matter and technique. Partly it must have been instinctive—the sound of the bird's song is formed by the shape of its beak—but it was certainly also a choice. This is striking in the observations of his brush, the subjects of simplicity, people and objects and landscapes of earth, of unpretentiousness and humility. And in the joy of his clean line, the celebration of colours, the jubilation of paints—as Afrikaans as only that mixture of Boer and Khoi and Oriental can be.

We live in futile times where the romantic impulse in gaudy theoretical garb (and a moralist stance), now ever more smothered in the garbage of 'post-modernism' and 'deconstruction', reigns supreme over Nomansland. We are terrorised by the notion of not being subtle enough to tease forth the shadows of 'meaning' or unconscious intentions hovering below the light of the surface—what, in older times, would have passed for 'soul' behind the mask of appearance. The fashionable discourse of mind-numbing, nit-picking academics sullies the clear waters of saying and singing and painting . . . François Krige's work points us in the salutary direction where paintings and drawings speak for themselves.

Painting is singing. Matisse says: "I continue painting until the hand sings." It is this hand-singing that François has left us, which we have the joy of listening to with our eyes.

Again, also, and at the risk of ruffling some rainbow feathers—in this colony where we are mortally afraid of being irrelevant or Eurocentrist (as if we don't all come from the same tradition of marking, making and transformation!), worried too about not being sufficiently committed or ironical or funny—there's more than a whiff of the stench of moral and emotional correctness. We are the victims of racism. Under cover of darkness we are dogs scrounging on rubbish dumps for the delicacy of a hand or two, to be chewed from the corpses thrown away there. Is the ultimate correct posture not death? Or suicide? Painting (and writing), on the contrary, when true to the deeper body, is *movement* ... François moves our eyes and our memories. He knows about the sounds of colours. One needs no formal apparatus to measure the depth of his empathy with his subjects, including the landscapes—with himself, the magic bird of hand and eye, as the vector of non-intellectual consciousness.

Like Cézanne he could have said that painting apples taught him about constructing the sky. And, like Uys, he knows about singing the sun. He too is a mystic of the surface: that most difficult of disciplines where touch and tone and knowing how not to go too far are all-important. But the sun can be dark at times—witness the Karoo funeral canvas as the tolling of a dark bell ...

Neither recluse nor iconoclast. Neither protestant nor puritan. Certainly no moralist. But with deep ethical concern grounded in his craft ...

MEMORY

The plateau is black and gleaming as if encased in dark glass. Wind never stops wailing. It peels the sky until it is white and burns the surface to barrenness. Here I wait for them. They make their way up from the misty valley. From quite far I hear, brought to me by the wind's coughs and sighs, the chatting of their voices. There are two parties. They carry bulging files under their arms, all the declarations and proofs, and virgin paper and pens and stamps, so that the new conclusions and sentence may be duly noted and officially certified. The first party hold: Now we have at last the occasion to complete the proceedings, too many aspects concerning your first trial were left in abeyance, black roots remained embedded and started festering, evil has to be extirpated, justice must triumph, the case *must* be closed with your execution. The world doesn't really have a past and a future; we live in a continuum (and a continuant) where there cannot be room for both guilt and expiation. The second party shift their robes over their shoulders so that the placating hands may slip more easily up the sleeves, and say: It is all very well, now the dreams may be extinguished, you have nothing to fear, your innocence will be made apparent once and for all. Like a beacon in the darkness. Tonight still you can come back home. *Home? Home?* When I look around, the phantoms have all dispersed. The plateau is black and gleaming and bare.

BIRTH

Sometimes a birth goes beyond death. I remember one of my cousins, Rachel Susanna. (There are several, with different family names—Stemmet, Burger, Cloete, Van Breda, Van Zyl . . .) This Rachel was born on a farm in the Bredasdorp district.

It must be a very dark night. The house is quiet with the stillness of an earth turning under a silent explosion of stars. Before daybreak, when the hushed blackness is even more profound, there is a shiver of wind in the poplars outside, like a breath reluctantly released. Is nobody else alive this wide night? These are the forgotten hours for dying and for being born. Everything is ready, the water has been heated, there are clean towels. There are two lamps—one by the bed, the other by the marble-topped washstand. The mother has given birth several times before, but this one is more difficult. She's so tired and dispirited. She will be assisted by the old brown woman who has brought her other children into the world as well. The midwife's hands were taught many years ago when she was still a slip of a girl by *old Missis* Keet of Montagu. One inherits kindness.

The labour pains seem to go on forever. Not a sound in the night—neither groan of floorboards nor handkerchief whisper of a bat under the eaves, nor even the faraway croak of a frog. Just heavy breathing and the suppressed moaning of the mother in the tousled bed.

Then, at last and suddenly, it is done: a sunburst of pain followed by the sensation of life slipping in one long loss from her womb. Exhausted silence.

The old brown woman has caught the small bundle deftly. Rapidly she does what is needed to separate mother and child. She then turns away, her back to the light. The woman in the bed already knows, no need to tell her.

The old midwife says with a low voice of infinite pity, her back still shielding the infant from the mother:

Ounooi, must I do it or do you want to do it yourself? There is no answer. Maybe it will by itself decide not to live.

She deposits the little blood-besmirched object on the cold surface of the washstand. The sharp contact with her buttocks jolts the child: a long, sobbing cry pierces the room's silence. Now, of course, there is no longer any question. Rachel Susanna is born with four tiny stumps instead of arms or legs.

Years later she is sometimes brought by her parents for a visit. She is a pretty and cheerful little girl with long honey-coloured curls. When I hear her coming down the passage with a shuffling sound (she quickly learns how to propel herself forward on her buttocks), I am frightened beyond words because I think it is the white parrot coming for me. I'm only reassured when she doesn't curse.

Rachel Susanna grows up to lead nearly a fully normal existence. She never acquires artificial limbs. She learns how to eat with a fork attached to one of her stumps by an elastic band. She is a beautiful woman. She talks and laughs a lot with a voice that seems to come from her nose. When she visits, my mother and she sing together. A man falls in love with her. She marries in a white gown with many pleats and frills. She is beautiful like an exotic parrot. Her husband carries her in his arms into the church as if for christening. There are any number of photos and articles of her in the newspapers. She conceives twins. She dies in childbirth. The twins, a boy and a girl, are healthy and strong.

MEMORY

Sometimes I have the impression that days and nights have come and gone, that tides have swelled and ebbed and moons bulged and shrank, that I have already blackened so many pages without realising what I wrote. Light is a wrinkle on the skyline, or it is an old story which has no end, a campsite where the coals never stop glowing. I wait here on the height, I don't know how long I have been waiting. I see from afar a person laboriously climbing up the path towards me, it may be a youth or an adult, woman or man, the person is wearing a long cloak. Maybe a duster coat. Because I'm standing motionless the dust doesn't incommode me. Dust is like the field of thoughts of somebody who is still alive. The person comes to where I stand waiting, he or she smiles wryly and holds out an oblong-shaped box. It is of a pale colour. It reminds me of the small box with the sliding lid in which I kept my pencils and my eraser and my one leaking pen when I was still at school. "This is your god," the person says. A quiet hand from a deep sleeve offers it to me. I take the box, slide open the lid: inside there's a slow chameleon, uncurled, big as a hand, so colourless that it might as well be transparent.

HERKLAAS

His name is Herklaas. (Hercules?) Local builder. The hands know bricks and plaster and paint. No, he doesn't work alone, he works for Attie. *Meneer* knows Attie Jass? Old man Jass, Attie's father, has six sons, they are all in the building trade. There's not a construction in

Ou-Dam, old or new, that has not been touched by the competent Jass family.

He sits on the low wall around Paradys' back stoep, bougainvillea throw a lacework of shadows on his face, behind him birds flit among the reeds in the river. His hands are big from labour; he often scratches his head, smiles.

He was born just on the other side of the river (he points), on the spot where Attie Jass built a big blue building for the rich owner of the guest house in town. He confirms that at his birth brown and white still lived together in Ou-Dam, with neither friction nor distinction. People were happy then. Somebody had a Decca record player, the kind that you wound up. Often the jollification continued right through the night, with daybreak everybody was *vaal* (grey in the face) from dancing.

We kept goats and chickens and ducks. Donkeys complained bitterly to the moon about being donkeys. People were poor and easygoing. But they didn't steal, no, they just took what they needed. The difficult thing in life is to stand up against the alcohol. A man must be able to take his responsibility.

There was not much else to do except dance and drink. Sometimes there was a film in town. The local chimney sweep announced the happy event with placard and bell. He was known as Drukjan (John Squeeze), because even if he was very thin, it still took a lot of pulling and pushing to get him through some of those narrow funnels. The children were scared and excited at the same time. He was the bogeyman; many a drunken father warned his brood to expect Drukjan to slither down the chimney pipe at night and enter their dreams with broom and with rope. Especially when the wind howled like that through the hole in the Poort. Nobody knew whether he was brown or white, he was that black with soot. Funny, in those days nobody asked. Then he walked down the street and clanged his bell and shouted: *Mooi bioscope! Mooi bioscope! Va-naand!* (Nice bioscope, nice bioscope tonight!)

The cinema was called Aalwyn Bioskoop (Aloe Bioscope) and it belonged to the Greek. Films were shown on Fridays and Saturdays. Ladies in hats and barefoot kids waited outside with copper coins in sweaty palms. On Monday morning the Greek conveyed his takings to the bank in a wheelbarrow. After some years he disappeared. The cinema was where Smittie now runs the Montagu Café, where one buys newspapers and milk and a Chinese mouth organ and wonderful aromatic, homemade apricot jam. Has *meneer* noticed how roomy it is inside? The only legacy of the defunct cinema is the videos one may rent from Smittie.

Much has vanished. People wandered off into the mountains after the baboons or started talking to the moon. Why, all those beautiful buildings in Swellendam also were built by *Slamse* (Islamic) craftsmen. They were old slaves, says Herklaas. And, admiringly: They could do whatever they wanted to with their hands! Are the houses not elegant? Then the money ran out and they too disappeared.

Has *meneer* heard the screaming peacock at the Eyssen house? If it weren't for the tail feathers I'd swear it's a madman crouching at that gate, shouting his shaven head off. Some people say it must be one of the freed slaves who died here, who wasn't buried properly. I don't know—Herklaas laughs and scratches his head. I have picked up a rainbow feather in the kloof, but I've also seen footprints.

And now? No, times have changed. He lives on the other side of Kanonkop (Cannon Hill, the ridge between Montagu and Ou-Dam, on top of which there is an ancient cannon mounted to point toward the Poort, just in case a commando of dusty and bearded Boere with wild eyes come thundering through from the interior). In the coloured section along the road which runs to the brickworks and the golf course, and on to the Keisie and Pietersfontein. When the National Party government forced the brown people out of Ou-Dam, they were obliged to sell up for next to nothing. His father cried black tears and died from an angry heart.

The new government wants to build houses for the poor. The project is called *masakhane,* "build one another." Middlemen will certainly steal the money. We are all victims of the past. The National Party buys over some of the councillors who represent the brown population; the National whites have tight lips and go to church on Sundays, but they still run the municipality as if it belongs to them.

In the brown location there is much drinking. It is dangerous to live there. People throw stones and fight with knives; they die for nothing, or just because they have seen a ghost. It is difficult to remain standing against death.

You asked me about the boy who died yesterday, *meneer?* He hanged himself. Nobody understands, but we all know why. He was a quiet boy. He even finished his homework before putting the rope around his neck. It was Walker who found him. *Meneer* knows Walker? He's that white man who is always walking up and down the streets of Montagu, with his hands behind his back . . . Yes, I have noticed the strange, well-dressed man with the grey hair, I often come across him in different parts

of town and at all times of the day, once I gave him a
lift to Robertson. He never seems to speak to anybody.

Herklaas looks out over the bending reeds and
laughs, showing his head in profile to the light. Yes, but
those whores waiting in the hot springs for their cus-
tomers: we call them brown dolphins. Aren't they
pretty?

TRANSITION

I have been putting it off. I close my eyes to the outside
world in order to see the rhythms and the shapes. Does
it help not to tell these stories? Do I understand this
land any better? But it is unfair. It is not *right* to bring
people to look and to look, and then expect them to
continue living as if they haven't seen. People turn their
glazed eyes to me. Who made the bed in which we must
now all lie down? This has always been a violent country. Rachel says: Oh no, one must pull a blanket over
one's head and hope nobody notices one is still here.
Hartman pours another drink with trembling hand.
Bruinman laughs to his heart's content and then frowns
fiercely. One is afraid of his eyes. Kwaaiman snorts: *Ja-
ja*, I told you so. Welcome to the rainbow nation!

From the night across the stifled river, maybe from
the dark bulk of Kanonkop over there, a pure white owl
arrives on the back stoep. It tries to find footing on the
bougainvillea pergola with a frantic beating of powerful
wings, it must be blinded by the light from the windows. I shout once and it flies off, nearly instantly invisible again in the darkness. Did it ever happen? I
relate the incident to a neighbour on the other side, a
very dark-skinned 'white' man with peculiarly blue eyes,

he knows everything and everybody in the neighbour-hood, one often sees him peering over hedges, he retired from the Railways. Maybe it is not a good omen, he says. Maybe owl is looking for snake. But it is not good if snake comes out at night.

In a seaside town not very far away a young woman is lured out of a nightclub by three young men. She knows one of them well. They wear their combs in their socks. They take her for a ride to a deserted stretch of undergrowth within hearing of the boomers. Among the bushes in the sand they rape her repeatedly. She screams in protest. They beat her and they beat her. One of them, the one she knows, takes out his knife and slits her throat and slashes open her belly. They leave her gurgling, they think she is already dead. She drags her mutilated body back to the road. She has to close the belly wound with one hand to prevent the innards from spilling out, she dares not move her head for fear of fatally severing arteries and windpipe. With her blood she writes the name of her attacker, the one she knows, on the tarmac. She tries to wave down passing motor-ists. People are afraid to stop at night. In the glare of headlamps people and animals in the dark have lumi-nous eyes.

A young man of seventeen needs money to take out his chérie, he wants to impress her with the city lights. His mother works as a domestic for white people in town. She leaves early and she comes home late. The young man sells his own younger brother, aged five, to some older men who must also make a living. He is given seventy Rand. It is not much, but it is the best they can do. Times are hard. He accompanies them when they take the child away from the ramshackle dwellings to a nearby rubbish dump. But only to watch.

The child feels chuffed to be taken notice of by grown men. The men start cutting up the child while still alive, for *muti*. The magical medicine will be more potent when hacked from a live human. In similar fashion it is believed that the only cure against AIDS is to sleep with a very young uncontaminated virgin.

During a telephone conversation Adam admits to not knowing what to do with Nietzke. Should he put her down or what? Yesterday when he gets up (he always rises very early in the morning to make coffee and to prepare his sandwiches for the day), Mercy is still in bed, her red hair like a pool of gossamer blood on the pillow, he's standing by the kitchen window mentally rehearsing the research work for the day ahead, there are absent voices in the archives, also to appreciate the sun lighting the roofs, and he sees Nietzke outside on the grass underneath the old fig tree. (The figs will be swollen and sweet this year if the starlings don't get there first.) Look high, look low. Nietzke is wagging her tail and worrying something with her wet teeth. Curiosity takes Adam outside to investigate, the dog doesn't want to give up its prize, first he thinks it is a glove, but then he sees to his horror that it is an infant's hand, limp and blue with a crust of blood, he cannot be sure whether it was a white or a black hand. He thinks the dog must have found this gruesome leftover on a rubbish dump in the vicinity. But is it only a leftover? The night soil of a dream? Are there more?

A boy of fourteen has a pistol. He comes home. His father finds him in the kitchen. The boy takes out the pistol and makes his father go down on his knees. Then he loosens his belt and drops his shorts. He puts the pistol to his father's temple and forces the man to commit fellatio with him. It is not yet lunchtime.

A man responds to a small ad in the newspaper of-
fering for sale a good table at a fair price. He goes to
the indicated address. A very old lady and her two quite
elderly daughters live in the house. The man inspects
the table. The price is reasonable, yes, but he sees tell-
tale small holes, the legs are infested with woodworm!
The black man says he wants to pay less, this table is
no good. The old white woman smiles in a superior way,
this is not up for bargaining, you can take it or leave it.
They argue. The man goes outside to his car and returns with a revolver. He shoots the old woman dead.
The two elderly daughters first scream and then push
their hands in their whimpering mouths. The man takes
them outside at gunpoint, he makes them get into the
boot of his car, he won't let just anybody sit in the car
with him, besides, this brace of old birds are making
squawking noises, he drives off with them, he doesn't
take the table. Not very much further, in the centre of
town, he stops and lets them out. He executes them with
one shot each right there on the street. In the struggle
one learned to shoot economically. One settler, one bullet!

A man with red-veined eyes and without a shirt manages to get into the house of an old widow. It is hot and
he is berserk. He clobbers her until she falls to the floor.
She is seventy-five years old. This is hard work. He
undoes his pants. But she wails: Don't do it, please! For
your own sake! I have AIDS!

My friend the sun poet (now in his grave) has a
daughter. The daughter has a grown-up son who still
lives at home, he is slightly retarded mentally. The son
is ill with acute pneumonia, he needs to be cared for in
hospital, he is taken to the local hospital, it is under new
management, other values now prevail, equipment is

carried off to be sold privately, one must understand that people are victims of racism. If the bosses can steal, why can we not help ourselves? It is early evening and the son is taken for his bath. The water is scalding hot. He is forced into the bath. He screams in pain, but he is slightly retarded mentally. The severe burns become infected, the infection complicated by bedsores. He dies from septicemia.

A man is arrested at the bus terminal in the city. He has travelled a long way from the countryside with an object wrapped in plastic on his lap. Sometimes he falls asleep. When he gets off the bus the object tumbles out of its wrapping, it is the chopped-off head of a small boy, the son of his sister, he is coming to the city to sell it for *muti*, life is hard in the interior, it is a tiring journey.

My friend the sun poet (now in his grave) has a daughter. She in turn has a grown-up daughter who is married with two children. They live in a Boland town where the white people are rich and arrogant and the brown people reside over the hill in an extension called Cloetesville. In the white town the wide streets are cooled by oak trees with cooing doves and furrows where water murmurs, the stately iron-roofed mansions are enclosed by low whitewashed ringwalls. In the coloured township the houses erected close to one another are painted in many colours, wind lives in streets littered with refuse, gang members who control the drug trade and militants of a Muslim organisation who want to drive out the Devil kill one another. Black people come in rattling, overloaded buses over the mountains from the east, they settle in squatter camps outside town, they slaughter goats and sometimes they burn a witch, somebody has to be responsible for death, their youths whiten their bodies with clay and live naked in the blue-gum plantations until such time as they are circumcised and can return to the community as men. The mayor of the town is black and of the ANC, because the white people are liberal, they have no memory of the past, there was no past, the past is just an ever-extending present. The husband of the sun poet's granddaughter employs as temporary gardener a black man from a close-by squatter camp. On his second day the gardener brings an accomplice to the house. There is too much work for two hands. They kill the old brown lady who has been with the family since birth and for generations. At lunchtime the mother (my friend's granddaughter) returns with the young boy-child. They kill the boychild. They force the woman to summon her husband home. Please, please, she says. When he arrives, they kill him. Then they wait. It is a long, hot and tiring day, they sit inside the cool house and they drink. They also smoke hemp to pass the time. *Dagga* makes time immediate by slowing it down. In the afternoon the bigger of the two children, the girl, comes back from school. She wears a school uniform and carries a satchel, her hair is plaited and blond. They rape the girl because they want the mother to tell them where the money is. Then they kill her. When they are tired they drink some more. Afterwards they rape the mother before they kill her. They also kill the dog, this is most difficult and messy. They use a hand axe and a big knife and a club. They leave with the family car and seventy Rand. It is not much but it will have to do, life is hard. When they run out of petrol they abandon the car in the informal settlement.

The regional magistrate says: It is a crying shame that an elderly woman at the ripe old age of 101 years should be raped, and so much worse when it is one's own biological great-grandmother who can no longer walk and who is half blind. The name of the accused is Kaandjie Aukus. His defence is that he confused her with a girl who caught his fancy. Earlier in the evening he courted her (the Afrikaans expression is: to whirr one's wing in the dust); she has red shoes, she's making eyes at him, he refers to her as a *donskoekie* (a downy biscuit), and she points out the wrong room to him. Later on in bed he realises he is mistaken in the nest. I was under the influence of strong drink and I could not distinguish the one woman from the other, he says. He is only eighteen years old, still wet behind the ears, life has not yet made him clever. It was dark, but when the complainant shouted he knew he had made an error. The complainant, who is half blind and has to be carried into court, gives a full description of how she was violated. She also offers the shout as evidence, so that the court may hear and be precisely informed. Women in this country demand justice to ensure their security, even if they shout, says Magistrate Sylvester Maïnga.

KOOS SAS

Koos Sas lies close to the surface for the Montagu population. Older people have in mind bits and pieces of the story, description they heard from their elders or picked up in the talk tree's shade. They exchange and amplify the bits and pieces and then they look uncomfortably at the dark face of the mountain. There are unlit rumours and restless memories in the rifts. The *ouvolk*, when chased away from the pools and the fountains, disappear that way behind rocky facades; they sit on their haunches in caves and look down upon the settlement with piercing eyes, in the gloom deeper in the shelters are magical paintings, these survivors still know how to dance the trance and when their hair stands on end and blood spurts from their noses they commune with the sacred animals; in passes roam ghosts of people who died when their carts plunged over precipices into ravines or who were ambushed by robbers or killed by leopards, still looking for a handkerchief or a letter lost in the struggle; there are fugitives and mad people singing to the wind over the black plateaux.

When I was small it was explained to me that I was found in the mountains. This is the way it works: In the fullness of time one's parents send somebody to fetch you, somebody like Koos Sas who runs fast and invisible like the wind and who is an inheritor of the old knowledge. He stays away a few days. He becomes one with the mountain, he breathes with the clouds, he crouches patiently behind a bush. He catches a small baboon. He brings the yelling animal back to the house where the midwife will prepare a tub of hot water. The captive's hair is scraped and its tail chopped off—and there you are, wrapped in a towel and ready to be presented to your mother! When I was bigger I could feel the hard knob of my coccyx where the tail was amputated. It meant that all the baboons still up there were camouflaged humans. Lucky too, not to be forcibly separated from their families.

People remember that Koos Sas had an insatiable appetite for meat. This would be his downfall. And, on top of it, he didn't like to work. No, he and work were mortal enemies, one inhabitant recalls. In the room of forgetting there's a newspaper clipping where one can see a smudged photo of Koos Sas: the captured prize is presented in a kneeling position, on each side a heavily

armed hunter holds up an outstretched arm so that
Koos Sas is given the appearance of being a vulture
having its wingspan measured, or a Viet Cong soldier
smoked out of a tunnel in the earth, or simply the cold
Che Guevara presented by peasant conscripts to the
camera for debunking and disenchantment.

In *Die Landstem* (The Country's Voice, a newspaper
of the period), dated 23 September 1950, Shane Cloete
recapitulates the story: Koos Sas has disproportionately
small and thick feet—with these he can travel long dis-
tances much more rapidly than any horse, while his di-
minutive stature stands him in good stead when he has
to hide. But he has an incredibly powerful neck.

He steals a rifle from *oubaas* Kriel of the Rooikrans'
farm. Constable Tonie Swanepoel is dispatched from
Montagu to apprehend the culprit. At that time Koos
Sas's wife is pregnant. Just before daybreak Swanepoel
surprises his man in a fold of the mountain where he and
his wife are regaling themselves with a leg of lamb spit-
sizzled over the discreet flames of a little fire of fortune.
Fat from the stolen animal still shines on their chins.

The thief is manacled. At a fast trot they start on the
road to town. Koos's wife cannot keep up and is left behind on the Anysberg farm belonging to the late *oom* Da-
vid Burger. At Almôrensfontein the captive is handed
over to the higher authority of Field-cornet Bennie Burger. Burger and Swanepoel are now on horseback; Sas
(who is allowed to take off his jacket before being hand-
cuffed again) continues on foot. With a mocking smile he
says over his shoulder: You can come now. I am ready.

When they reach *Hoek van die Berg* (Mountain's Corner) the two horsemen have to use their spurs ever more
frequently if they don't want to be left behind by the
nimble runner. As luck would have it, they meet the late

oom Barend Geldenhuys in his horse cart bringing a column of dust down the road. They all climb aboard, Sas is sitting between them, the two mounts have their reins fastened to the back of the cart.

Scarcely has he been released from prison than Koos Sas lays low another sheep in the Keisie. One short bleat of agony and then the voice is blood. The lure of mutton is irresistible. Constable Swanepoel tracks him down in the Boontjiesrivier settlement and locks him up. Chunks of half-raw meat are presented in court as evidence. Koos Sas is given the jacket—that is, declared an habitual criminal and accorded an indefinite sentence of hard labour. Together with other 'bandits' he works in the Keina River under guard of one Robert Rowe. The very first morning he manages to get a bush between Rowe and himself and off he goes. Breasting the first ridge he stops, throws his hands in the air and shouts loudly: Look at me one last time, I greet you, ha-ha-ha-ha!

A few days on he is caught once again in the Ceres district, where Swanepoel goes to fetch him. (It must be noted that these localities are quite a distance apart; Koos Sas must either be ubiquitous or else propel himself through the air.) Now he is escorted to prison in George, close to the smoking ocean, where he will be building roads.

He is discharged after some years of breaking bigger stones into smaller stones, whereupon he returns to Montagu. By now he is a toughened man, still with the same ravenous lust for meat and, as well, with no trace of mercy for his own kind. At Hoek van die Berg, Boetatjie Botha runs a small store. Boetatjie is not of an impressive height either, and besides, he is a bachelor. Koos is looking for work. Boetatjie, his upper body barely jutting above the counter, reluctantly employs Koos.

Boetatjie has to leave on an errand. When in the late afternoon he returns, he is most displeased with the services of his hired help, he pays him and shows him the door (literally—*steek hom in die pad*, sticks him in the road). Koos is not at all happy. He is furious because Boetatjie curses him and calls him a *Touwsrivier Boesman* (presumably an insult even though we have lost the implication). But he hides his fury by looking away to the mountain.

First Koos goes to sit in the shade of a pepper tree some distance away. The sun is white. Then he returns to the store (which is already closed), he taps on the door, he wants to purchase flour, he asks nicely. Three pounds is weighed out on the scales, Koos wants more, Boetatjie bends down to scoop more flour from the bag. *"Met hierdie beweging moes hy die dood op die mees boosaardige wyse tegemoetgaan."* (With this gesture he was to encounter death in the most black-hearted way.)

With a length of sturdy wood Koos clubs him so violently that blood spurts and splatters to the ceiling. Koos cuts his victim's throat with his sharp sheepskinning Joseph Rodgers knife. He beheads Boetatjie. He puts the head on the counter so that passersby may think the owner is just daydreaming. He takes the dead man's clothes, they are about the same size, and then he goes away.

Boy Hugo arrives late at night at the closed store on his way home from drunkenness, he clumsily creeps up to the loft by the outside stairs, one doesn't want to disturb the storekeeper, he sleeps the sleep of one who has had his fill of bad wine, only the next morning does he notice something amiss, there are too many flies in Boetatjie's mouth, he gallops off to go call the police. A horrendous sight meets their eyes.

Constable Swanepoel leads the enquiry. At one of the workers' cottages he is told about an unknown *Boesman* who spent last night sleeping out there behind a big bush next to a little fire like an eye or a fallen star. At another cottage an old brown woman with one hand above her milky eyes says it is the same Bushman who ran so fast that day in front of the constable and another *baas* over the plain of Spitskop. The horses cannot catch up with the wind, as dust be my witness.

Koos, meanwhile, goes to Touwsrivier, where he buys a train ticket for Cape Town. At the station he pretends he earned the money by building dams. There are never enough dams in this thirstland, the sheep are not as fat as they used to be.

His presence has been noticed and signalled. Constable Piet Jonker leaves by train from Ashton to try and catch up with him. Looks high, looks low, no luck. From Cape Town, Koos Sas travels to Spes Bona, where his wife is now residing. He makes love to her when it is dark and also when it gets light. He continues on his way and at Wolseley, as he walks along the railroad track, he sees Piet Jonker in the train going by. Koos "makes himself out of the feet"—in other words, he takes to his heels. He returns to his wife. She says— No, but Koos, you must go, my man; the police were here looking for you.

Some people say he moves through the veld with the baboons, he speaks their tongue fluently, but because he has stolen so many of their kind they don't warn him about his persecutors. In the Worcester district he is recognised, trying to run low the way baboons do. A farmer traps him, using a tethered sheep as bait, and delivers him to the field-cornet. He is put in the field-cornet's cart and now he will be taken to the police. It gets dark and Koos asks if they may stop so that he can stretch his legs. He needs to piss. Hardly does he hit the ground before he's running, all the field-cornet hears is a snapping of branches, and Koos is away! His tiny hands easily slip through the handcuffs. Fierce fire-tongues bark from the officer's revolver into the night. Bark here, bark there: to no avail.

But the very next night the fugitive is caught again and put behind bars in Worcester's gaol. Constable Tonie Swanepoel comes from Montagu to stay with Koos, right in his cell. Sas asks Swanepoel whether he's sure his tail has really been cut.

The case is brought to court in Montagu. All the available firearms in town are snapped up. So many people try to get into the courtroom that the door is torn from its hinges. The crowd at the entrance becomes more and more compact; one lady faints and is nevertheless carried into the room by the surging mass of bodies, she will be following the proceedings the whole day and be taken home tonight without remembering a word of what happened; another has her hat pushed over the eyes but she can do nothing since her arms are pinned to her body. I am blind! she shouts. And: The blood of Boetatjie Botha calls out for vengeance!

Koos Sas lies, whistling through his teeth like the deceptive wind in the high mountains. He is a pale chameleon in the box. Only his eyes move. Magistrate van Alphen finds him guilty. For sentencing he has to appear before a judge in Worcester. Tonie Swanepoel knows his man. Are they not old acquaintances? He will take Koos to Worcester. He will put him in a cell with other convicts, for safety. Koos doesn't smell of the veld anymore, and there's a girl who works at the post office whom Swanepoel wants to visit.

Ah, but this very night Koos Sas escapes together with two other prisoners. They tear their blankets into strips to lower themselves from the roof. He is the last one to go, his newfound friends hold open a blanket below for him to jump in. But they are weak from their incarceration and Koos falls with a thud to the earth. He is injured. The leg may be broken, the wonderful feet are numb. Hobbling as best he can, he follows his accomplices in their flight towards the river.

Two of them walk right through: they will be caught tomorrow morning. Koos, however, is wily as the walk-softly (chameleon), he stays in the water and makes his way upstream until he reaches the foothills where the ground becomes hard and bare like glass.

He flees to a farm in Namakwaland. (This must be at least five hundred kilometers away, and his body is broken.) His photo is placarded all over the territory. Koos Sas is a proscribed outlaw, he may be shot on sight.

On January the 8th, 1922, Constable Jurie Dreyer arrives on patrol at the Droodaap farm near Springbok. The farmer is out in the veld with his labourers. We are within earshot of the eternal silence of the great desert on the other side of the Gariep. The islands in the Gariep (Orange River) are the traditional and last refuges for outlaws, diamond smugglers, deserters, rebel Khoi headmen who are now raiders.

A photo falls from Dreyer's pocket. The farmer picks it up and jokes: Is this your girlfriend? Dreyer blushes. The farmer looks more closely, recognises Koos Sas. He covers up by turning his back. He asks Koos to go fetch a bucket of water. But Koos is no fool, by now his nose will warn him of a bad-intentioned Boer a mile away. So he disappears

Koos returns to fetch his meagre belongings. The

people on the islands will not be generous to a poor fugitive. The constable has borrowed the farmer's gun, he is waiting in ambush. Koos stops, he sniffs the air, smiles, and he runs to a nearby hill (the original is: "he chooses the rabbit-path").

Constable Dreyer is on his horse, he rides to the other side of the hillock as fast as his horse will carry him. Koos doesn't fear horses. But his body is tired. He squats on his haunches behind a low bush on the hillside to watch the distant farm. He rubs his small feet. To-night he will collect his possessions. The wind is in his face. It carries such a sweet, dry desert smell of freedom.

Constable Dreyer dismounts, he climbs the hill from the other side, against the wind. He comes up behind Koos. A twig cracks. Koos looks around. The constable aims and pulls the trigger, and when smoke spurts from the barrel Koos Sas, 'the infamous killer', exhales his last breath. (Take a good look—here I go, ha-ha-ha!)

His skull is considered to be so typical of the "pure Bushman race" that it is sent to the University of Stellenbosch for study.

It is later returned to Montagu. Nobody wants it. The Reverend Boesak's daughter comes to the museum to ask for the relic. It belongs to her people, she says; it deserves proper burial. The curator's blue eyes are very big behind her glasses. The skull? Oh that one! Now where could it have gone?

GERT APRIL

At night, with shadows dancing on the thin walls covered by old newspapers, like ghosts leaving no marks on the pages of history, people tell stories about Koos

Sas and Gert April. They are folk heroes. One could say they are resistance fighters. How else can you die when there is no hope of redress? People softly pass these tales from mouth to mouth, painting the pictures in roundabout ways. Except when they're drunk—then they get incoherent. Sometimes they fall down laughing in broad daylight, and the whites don't understand why.

It is said that Gert April (also known as Gert Kaffer) warned the police every time about the exact place of his next strike; even so they never succeeded in catching him. One day he surprises a boy walking about in the veld with a gun, he overwhelms him and runs off into the mountains with the firearm. He is a deadly sure shot, killing as he goes along. He executes Barend Geldenhuys's carthorse. He slays an elderly brown worker and his wife in cold blood. He put to death the *boerboel* of Tonie Swanepoel.

On the Onderkruis farm Gert April plays a game of cat and mouse with the owner, *oubaas* Fourie. This continues for months. It is April's heart-wish to put a bullet through the farmer's head, but he just can't get in that one fatal shot. Is it because of an old grudge, a wage dispute? Or are they otherwise related? Who knows?

April lies in wait among the rocks of a hill overlooking the farmhouse. Whenever old man Fourie leaves the house, he has to dash from oak tree to oak tree until he can skip out of the line of fire behind the corral. Small plumes of dust grow instantly around his feet. The old fellow becomes so agile, moving in hops and bounds, that he becomes known as Ritteltit (Jitters) Fourie. When he makes it to town for the once-a-month Sunday communion (a long sip of free wine), young rascals sneak up behind him to bang a blown-up paper bag, just for the hilarious fun of seeing old farmer Fourie jump and run for the nearest tree. But it is a bothersome business, one cannot answer all of nature's calls inside the house, and constant ducking and streaking loosen the bowels even more.

A *baster* (a person of mixed origin considered more white than brown) named Piet Alexander saves Fourie's life. By now April has been declared an outlaw, there's a reward of thirty pounds to whoever brings in his head, dead or alive.

Alexander (also a fine shot) one day runs into April in Langkloof. How are you? I'm just fine, and you? No, nothing to complain about. The family? Healthy, by the grace of God. Yours? Same . . .

The two men size each other up. Alexander challenges April to a shooting competition. The target is the skull of a cow. They set it up a good distance away. The one who succeeds in knocking it over must go and put it back. Cocksure Gert Kaffer—a braggart, *windmaker*, as we say in Afrikaans—fires first, and it's a bull's-eye. As he swaggers away to go and right the target, Piet Alexander lifts his gun and shoots him in the back between the shoulder blades.

Alexander never receives his thirty pounds recompense. There's a certain reluctance. People turn their faces away and say, *ja-nee*. The general feeling is that he shouldn't have gunned down his adversary from behind. Kenneth Knipe's grandfather buys April's gun at the court sale for half a crown.

MEMORY/FATHER

My father runs from the burning house with only his pyjamas on. Because it is night and smoke blackens the scene, and because my father stands out in silhouette against the backdrop of flames, I think at first that the dark smudges on his nightclothes must be burn spots. But when he comes nearer, so close that I can distinguish his grey hair and the fright in his eyes, when he falls down repeatedly and gets up again with great difficulty, and when the stains start spreading, glistening to the naked eye, then I know it is blood. Blood also dribbles from his mouth, flowing over chin and neck to dirty the jacket even more. I call out loudly: most probably he cannot hear, what with the snapping and crackling and popping of the burning background. Still he keeps trying to come towards me. I want to rush up to him, I want to cradle his grey head, but the firemen keep a very tight grip on my arms just above the elbows.

THUNDERSTORM

It is hot as hell. Towards afternoon dark clouds rise in pillars behind mountain ranges to the north. Wind. A distant drumming coming closer. From the Karoo, then through the Koo, thunderstorms arrive with advance drummers covered in dust and perspiration. Dancing lightning as if treading on thorns, flashes where God is taking pictures in the penumbra (and there's nothing to be seen), etchings, curses, bursts, fits, whiplashes, knots, clubs, thuds, orgasms, old-fashioned sparks from tinderboxes, electric shudders. Just before the clouds break it is hot and humid so that one's skin crawls with pearls of sweat, then a draught of cooler air, and only afterwards the splashing and clattering of big rain. It is lucky that no stones are thrown—some farmers in the Koo and up the Keisie Valley only last week had the

young fruit in their orchards ruined by hail. There is
no protection for the wings of birds. It goes dark. First
the emergency switch of the house trips a few times.
Suddenly all the electricity in town fails. Drops rustle
on the iron above—we are cooped up inside the rain—
and in places the roof starts leaking. Whenever there's
a pause all the birds chirp and chatter and coo and caw
and trill and twitter and cheer from swollen breasts.
Frogs run amuck, there are fierce eructations in the
marshes. But right around us lightning chains still
tremble and jitter their slashing dance. Sometimes a
news flash will briefly expose a mountain-sleeve. Streets
and houses are quiet, expectant, dark. Here and there
the halo of a candle behind a pane. Our sleep is restless—probably because of the ceaseless clattering over
our heads—and I dream my own death, throttling, a
snake shedding its skin. Waking up is a catch in the
throat. Will the waters rise and come screaming like a
mad train engine through one of those gaps in the
mountain? Where have the snakes gone? My grandfather left some scribbled observations (prophecies?) in
the margins of the Holy Book; the truth will not be
manifest because too many pages have gone up in
smoke.

The whole world smells fresh. A mixture of sweet
and earthy and spicy, of leaf and shrub and flower. The
house is full of insects—beetles and bugs, moths, mosquitoes, gnats, even a dragonfly seeks shelter and now
pretends to be a helicopter in the shower booth. In the
street snails and slugs are out for a suck-footed stroll,
frogs have been flattened, geckos and lizards drown
washed up against blocked drains. A feast is awaiting
the ants. They will live up to expectations. Deconstruction is an act of creation when everything is dragged

back into the earth. Malachite sunbirds flit through the air in pursuit of all this food on the wing, like switchboard operators harassed by too many calls. Just as long as the current doesn't trip once again. Sugarbirds flutter, disappointed by all the flower cups knocked senseless and limp by successive showers. Fog banners drape the lower mountain-slopes: old blue men sleep with their beards above the sheets.

Early on I go running in the kloof, hop-skip-jump-sloshing over new gulleys of garrulous brown mountain water. Dassies (rock rabbits) are not out yet; they're a retiring species of mammal waiting for the sun to warm their movements. A black eagle is however already on the lookout for feed, croaks, rises twice from just in front of me, the wingspan nearly two meters, and climbs in a vertiginous ascent along the sheer rockface—an inaudible thunderstorm over the face of the sun. Up to six breeding pairs have been spotted in the vicinity. One doesn't startle any small buck this time, but one hears their whistling echoing through the chasms. I won't encounter any baboons either, there is too much to feast on in the mountains, it is only during the dry season that they descend to plunder the gardens and throw stones at people. And leopards are far too shy. They follow the baboons. Later a few Egyptian geese fly high over a marsh of rushes, hooting hoarsely. Again it rains, but softer now. A bushel of dead moths is thrown out on the roof to dry, if only the sun would break through the drizzle. Still later five small brown boys come to sprint hither and thither in the open under the trees of Lovers Walk, right up to where the mountain frowns its eyebrows around the entrance to Donker Kloof (Dark Canyon). There is the sentinel farmhouse, with the desperate slave disguised as a peacock screaming invective at a lost past, squatting on the gate with its long tail of sunlight-by-night. The boys utter short, sharp cries. Barefoot they run after a little white ball in the wet grass. There are gaps in time. One's youth is forever, it never passes, surfaces suddenly when the heavens split or when the river is in flood with tree trunks and dead donkeys and ostriches in its foaming brown maw. Progress comes and goes. A generation is blinded by the muck on television. It doesn't matter. For all at once a cloud takes fire, the veld is heavy with smells, the dove's breast throbs with hooping sounds— and the world is young and untamed, a tumbling planet through the times of a veiled sun.

BIRDS

Plant by plant, Lotus shapes the garden around the cottage. She also spots and remembers the many birds which inhabit our environment; shrubs are carefully chosen because they provide berries for our winged visitors. Close by there are rock or speckled pigeons with eyes like red seeds; feral pigeons; ordinary Cape turtle doves; the rare laughing dove (called the red-breasted or lemon dove in Afrikaans), still chuckling at the jokes it was told by my mother; malachite sunbirds (the evocative Afrikaans name is *Jangroentjie*, Johnny Green) with their jackets of viridian silk; paradise flycatchers as small multi-hued sword-fighters ...

High in the belhambra a green-and-white *meitjie*, Klaas' Cuckoo, cheeps for days on end. It is supposed that the bird was given its European name after Klaas, a Khoi in the service of François le Vaillant, who was an avid explorer through the Cape interior of the last century. This Frenchman took a cock with him wherever he went, as alarm clock; his wife was a Hottentot. Maybe the bird is still longing for Klaas and trying to imitate the feathered clock.

Streaking out of the sea of reeds, stopping to show off by riding a stem as if it were a swing, are masked weavers and stately red bishops; even the odd kingfisher. The mountain seems to be the huge mansion of African spoonbills, of yellow-billed egrets and little egrets and great white egrets all looking for cattle to bring them their ticks as sustenance, of watchful jackal buzzards and hadedah ibises—who punctually announce sundown by flying low up the valley and angrily shouting: "The end is coming! The end is coming!"

And when we take some rubbish to the municipal dump outside town, where poor people with ragged clothes pick over the refuse, we come across a colony of graceful sacred ibises (known as *skoorsteenveërs*, "chimney sweeps") walking on fastidious stilts, pretending not to notice where they are.

MEMORY/MOON

The moon waxes and it wanes. When it is hollow (sliced in half) the *ouvolk* say dead people are living in its belly. But mostly dead people go down into a hole in the earth. Shamans in a trance also descend into the depths to visit the rain bull; but they don't really die, although they may be lifeless like flower heads after strong rain. Maybe it is not the hole of the truly dead. Big Snake goes down into the hole—to mess with Rain Bull. Is it from anger that the earth then vomits a flood? One must placate these forces. One should be like *Heitsi Ei-*

bib, the magician who can change his shape whenever he needs to, and slip away unnoticed. Even Death will have to look for you in many places. We know Heitsi Eibib dies time and again in many different places, to be reborn in another form. His graves are all over the country. Like a good Bushman he sits in the earth with his knees drawn up to his chin, and he has his arrows and softened skins with him. It brings good luck to the traveller to pass by a grave and add a pebble to the pile of stones there, or to leave a branch, some clothing, maybe a skin of his own.

One observes the moon being reborn again and again. It is like reading a book with the words as spirits changing shape. Somewhere I read that the year starts with August rains for the ancient Khoikhoi inhabitants. August is called *broad green*, because it is the time of grass and flowers; September is *shit moon*; October is *speckled ear*, when the veld begins to dry; November is *eland's moon*, because this is the month when these potent, quasi-human bucks will mate; December is *little eland*; January, *great eland*; February is *star death*; March is *twisted ears*, the dassies have their young; April is *crooked fire*, now the veld is bare and the people go hungry; May is *black moon*, as the grass begins to grow again; June is *pale moon*, and the grass and flowers are good; July is *chewing wood*: the first cold sets in.

MEMORY/RUNNER

In the kloof, on my way back from the early-morning jog (a klipspringer jumps up hardly three yards in front of me, it is grey and has small horns, stands frozen for a split second and looks at me with dark eyes, then flees up the steep mountainside, jumping, hooves together, from rock to rock), I unexpectedly meet another runner coming around a bush. A well-aged man, clad only in shorts, with a long staff. He's running barefoot. He is tanned and fit, muscles show under the skin even though it is an old man's body. The hair is cut short and he has a severely trimmed grey beard. Then I notice something wrong. He carries one hand curled in an unnatural position before his chest, a dead flower, a shrivelled chameleon, and in his run there's something of a stumble, as if one leg could be a little slow. (But the body seems to be symmetrically developed.) Are these the sequels of a long-ago stroke? Did he have polio as a child? We nearly run into one another. He is as surprised as I am. I greet him. He emits a friendly something, and it comes out a mumble, as if there could be a speech defect, a tongue too heavy for words. Ten yards on I look around, already he has vanished between some shrubs behind the line of reeds. And later on the stoep I keep watch for his return, to no effect. Would my father have looked like this if he had recovered from his paralysis? There was something archetypically familiar in his eyes. Further back? My grandfather? Where is he going? Is he not coming back this way?

CLEFT

I promise Gogga that we'll go walking in the mountains and swim in a cool pool, the way I did as a child. But I want to warn her against becoming attached to this land. One is enchanted by the rhythms and spaces of one's youth, the landscapes of innocence and of joy. It is good that these should exist. They give you room to wander through later in life, they demarcate your dreams and provide them with resonance. But choose some other part of the world, I want to say—take the Mediterranean or an island or some fortified town or a city with parks and museums. Become attached elsewhere. Go lose your blameless heart to ice floes, or Fire Earth, or Rimbaud Rainland. We are painted in the colours of disappearance here. At best we are destined to become other (while even now not knowing who we were): it is 'good' in a practical and possibly a moral sense, but it is painful. Above all, don't let this décor, these expanses of light and darkness, enter your memory. Look at the surroundings as pleasant postcards; let not this shimmering snake of a river soak your imagination, close your eyes so that these mountains cannot rise and imprint themselves upon the backs of your eyes as fortresses of transcendence, be careful not to allow the ocean to lay down patterns of an interior rhyme, don't look at the fire in the clouds and rather pretend that you can neither see nor hear nor smell the wind. Do not let any of these odours become as familiar as forgetting. We are only visiting here. It must die away.

With Lotus, Gogga shares her intimate secrets, maybe the heartache of a relationship that doesn't work out, a little boyfriend lured away by a competitor, a friend who is no longer a friend, a teacher who has made her cry . . . She questions Lotus about all the forms of secret knowledge that a girlchild must learn in order to survive in a world conceived and controlled and made horrible by men.

When we are alone, though, she and I, she takes it upon herself to discuss weighty matters (like placating the ogre)—poetry or philosophy or the ways of the world. Or she may ask: What's the difference between

an Afrikaner and an Englishman? And I answer: Afrikaner children don't wear shoes.

We walk into the kloof when the afternoon is still
hot, before the air ripens to darker hues. She holds my
hand tightly, there are long silences, the rocks and the
pebbles of the riverbed are not easy on her bare feet,
she thinks carefully before uttering serious reflections.

She knows the story of Ariadne kept prisoner in the
Minotaur's labyrinth, of how Theseus saves her by slic-
ing off the man-bull's head with his knife, but he has to
do it with eyes closed because if one were to look into
the animal's eyes one would be shamed, and when they
sail back to their city Theseus attaches the head to the
ship's mast and blood drips on the sails, making them
black, and the king is in his tower looking to see if
they're coming, a servant blows the horn. When the
king sees the head nailed to the mast, he gets such a
fright that he jumps into the harbour. His coat is too
heavy, it drags him down. The fishes find comfort in his
pockets.

She knows the story of Icarus who wants to fly too
high, who doesn't listen to his father, his wings are
scorched and he falls from the sky into a beehive.

She knows the story of Christ killed with a pistol by
bad people who do not like his message, that he is put
away in the earth, but he only pretends to be dead and
after three days he gets up to go home.

Whether he is a god? But God is just a thought. She
thinks for a long while ... God is a thought of nature.
The idea is born with each person and dies with each
person. One could say God is Nature. We only live
thanks to the trees which give us oxygen. If it hadn't
been for trees we'd long since have died from pollution.

Look, she says, Nature is very angry with the French

at present, that's why they have droughts. Why is he annoyed? Because when the French come to Africa they can do what they want and go wherever it pleases them to go, but in France the 'maroon' people suffer all sorts of restrictions, there are many things they are forbidden to do, the gendarmes always bother them for their 'papers'.

She knows about praying. She prays for the family not to die. She prays for a tortoise. She wants to send a postcard to Grandfather Oubaas and Grandmother Ounooi (my parents), she knows they are in heaven. All that is needed is the means to get it to them. How shall we do it? A rocket could take it as far as the moon. They will then come and fetch it there. She says she would so much like to be small again, so as to forget about her dead family. When she was little she was happy because she didn't know. Now that she knows, she finds it impossible to forget.

We finally come across a pool deep enough to wade in. The bottom is murky. I warn her to be careful— there may be pieces of metal or glass, maybe even a rusty motorcar brought here by the flood or chucked into the river by careless people. If one opens the earth, one risks getting cut. I also tell her not to drink the water (she's very thirsty)—it is more than likely polluted.

Most of the heat is gone from the afternoon when we turn back on our way to Paradys. Soon the hadedah ibises will fly in pairs into the kloof, cawing awful imprecations through hooked bills. A group of barefoot brown boys come sprinting from the reeds. Look! Look! Gogga says excitedly—Afrikaners! One of them is whimpering in pain, tears have streaked the dust on his cheeks. They must have been fishing. The one in pain has a fishhook embedded in his finger. I take him home, leave Gogga with Lotus, and drive the boy to the dispensary in town to have the hook removed.

Afterwards I accompany him to the part of town where he lives. Children play cricket in dusty streets, a drunken man walks with his body absurdly tilted, dogs gambol on a rubbish tip, vegetables in the gardens seem wilted, boxlike houses have crudely painted names: *Bankrot-maar-Windgat* (Bankrupt but bragging), *Spook-en-Spartel* (Struggle and thrash).

Back at Paradys, Gogga is jumping up and down with excitement. Lotus has found a tortoise in the garden. They are to call it Belle. It is medium small and polished, withdraws its head, waits for our excitement to pass, looks at us with a questioning and shiny eye, heads off for fresh food as soon as it can.

Apparently there are thirty-nine different kinds of tortoise in the world, nine of them can be found in the Cape Colony and three live only here. The largest is known as the "leopard" or mountain tortoise, which can grow to a length of sixty centimeters and weighs up to forty-five kilograms. The smallest, on the other hand, is the *Homopus signatus,* barely ten centimeters long and weighing in at one hundred fifty grams—its shell is of a reddish salmon colour with black spots. The rarest of these prehistoric thoughts with their petrified shields of understanding, content to munch their way through the world, is the *suurpootjie* (sourfoot, also known as the geometrical tortoise, *Psammobates geometricus*) with its pattern of yellow lines on a dark shell. The only cry ever emitted is by the male, during intercourse, as if he were angry or in pain.

On weekend days groups of people arrive by car and stop on the open grassland of Lovers Walk. They play games, they spread blankets and have meals, they lean back their heads to let the wine gurgle down their gullets, they turn up the music on their car radios and then they dance to the thump and the blare, they shout and they guffaw. The big mountain tortoises which live on the Eyssen farm sometimes meditatively graze their way right into town. We don't dare tell Gogga about the seven gentle giants who were martyred last week: turned upside down and kicked, stoned until the shells cracked, their eyes gouged out. Four of them had to be put out of their misery. Nobody knows who did it— drunken revellers? disorientated kids? people afraid of the tortoise's purported magic? The municipality announces a reward for any information that might lead to the apprehension of the delinquents.

OOM APPELTJIE

Here, the day before yesterday, the eighty-one-year-old Absalom Hartzenberg (much better known as Oom Appeltjie—Uncle Little Apple) died after going to bed with a cigarette for company. He was tired from a morning's hard drinking and needed to contemplate the wisps of smoke. Oom Appeltjie was paralysed from the waist down, he moved around in a wheelchair which he used to block the parked cars of visitors to the town until they gave him a tithe. In 1993 he was found guilty of driving his wheelchair under the influence of strong liquor, he was forbidden from ever again wheeling himself down a public road, a sober person must accompany him at all times. The police said that the lady who looked after him, Charlene Abdul, returned to her own home when Oom Appeltjie decided to go and rest. At about 4

P.M. she heard anguished cries for help, she rushed out and saw smoke, when she got to him his bed was in flames. He is survived by six foster children.

TRICKSTER

This is what I tell Gogga: Look around you. What do you see? There's a moon and there are stars; there are trees and shrubs and rocks. These are all petrified shamans, subterranean travellers, wind-runners, death dancers who change themselves into rocks and antheaps, etc., to become invisible to the others who invade this land. They are very patient. But they have been waiting such a long time that they've forgotten they're not trees and stars, etc.

The Khoisan say they are descended from 'the people of the early race'. These *ouvolk* are nearly like men and women; they walk in a stooped way only because they don't want to be taken for humans in this violent country. Time comes nearer, though, so that those with animal names become the animals whose names they possess and the others become men and women. At that time real people obtain fire. With fire comes understanding, which leads to memory, and therefore death comes into the world. Do you remember how Icarus was stung to death by bees swarming like sparks around him? Well, the 'God' (the I-dea) of the Khoisan, Heitsi Eibib, the one who is buried in many graves, has a similar experience. He takes too much honey from the bees. They punish him by biting off part of his skull. (These shards and pieces of skull were found in the earth by paleontologists to prove the existence of upright-walking hominids millions of years ago.) Heitsi Eibib tricks his niece, Dassie, she thinks he wants to give her honey; he kills her and from her fur he fashions a hood for his open head. And when his wives revolt against the greedy rule of man, they pull off this hood, so there he stands all vulnerable and humiliated with bees swarming around the gaping wound. Oh, he plucks out his brains (to stop the buzzing and the burning?) and scatters them left and right—and two kinds of *uintjies*, bulbous staple food, grow up: the sweet and the bitter.

What she should really know though, are the stories about Kaggen. Kaggen is both of the 'early people' and of the real people. He can be a magician, but also stupid. He is the trickster god, and yet he speaks like a child. Kaggen (often referred to as the Mantis) takes on the form of a dead *hartbees*. Girls find him and cut him up to take him home. The chunks of flesh are like bees or like live coals. While they carry their miraculous find, the head—in the hands of the youngest girl, the prettiest one—starts whispering: Please remove the thong from my eye, child, it hurts me so. The other girls do not believe her story. When the head speaks again, louder this time, with a mellifluous voice, the young girl drops her load, whereupon it shouts: *Eina!* (Ouch!) All the girls now throw down their meat and run home, where there is nothing to eat. Kaggen's parts join together again, he becomes a man and he chases them. He catches the beautiful one, the young one who caressed his head, and takes her to his house. When the girl prepares his private parts as food, they spring into her. Kaggen shouts: Oh, I have tasted the girl that nobody has tasted!

Then there is revenge... Kaggen puts a piece of his son-in-law's shoe in a pond and a tiny eland is born from it. Oh, how Kaggen loves his eland! Every day he secretly feeds it honey. The other animals die, because the veld is dry. Also, there's no longer any honey for the family because the trickster takes it all. So the family send a grandchild to spy on him and when the boy tells them what he sees, they wait until Kaggen is away looking for honey, and they kill the eland. The meat is delicious on the tongue and they are starved. Kaggen returns with his skin-bag heavy with sweetness, he calls and calls for his eland. Nothing. When he finds the bloodstains, he weeps.

When he finds the bloodstains, he weeps. It is evening near a station in a suburb of Cape Town. A man grabs a woman and drags her off to the nearby bushes, he half undresses her and forces himself upon her. When he is spent she bends over swiftly and tears off his penis with her teeth.

MEMORY/TREE

The robust man with the bald head (except for some reddish fluff) who comes to look at the house stands for quite a while under the talk tree. Bees are humming insistently. Maybe the expression on his face is not wonder, but sadness. Some men, when they are very sad, frown their foreheads. He remembers events which he never shares with anybody. He knows things which he doesn't remember.

His mother comes from a poor family. They live as tenant farmers on a piece of arid land outside town. This house here belongs to Sleepgat Swanepoel, the cripple. Swanepoel is not young anymore, and he's looking for a wife. At least he has a house and a donkey. He can provide.

The poor family give their young daughter to the disabled bachelor. And he starts turning her over, ploughing the furrow, planting the seeds. One after the other she gives birth to ten children, this stout man-child is the tenth. So when she is pregnant once again and for the eleventh time, totally exhausted and horrified by the never-ending life progressing from her belly, she waits until dark, the man is not yet back from the bar in Bath Street, and she goes outside and hangs herself from the tree which looks like an elephant. The bees sing even at night.

It is said that the cripple returns home drunk, shouts for his wife, falls asleep. It is only with the light of day that the woman with the huge belly and the naked feet is found swinging from a branch. The child inside her is dead also. Bees have not touched her body.

HANGING

I don't know how true this story is, Kwaaiman says. Maybe there's a mistake in the name. *Ja-ja.* But what I *do* know is that life in this country takes funny turns. I went to visit friends of mine near Vrotkop last weekend, he continues. They told me of this weird fellow who always walks hands behind his back along the roads. Sometimes he is seen in Ashton, then in Bonnievale or Robertson, well-dressed but never talking to anybody. They say his name is Walker. They also say he was caught one day exposing himself to some young brown girls near Vrotkop (when it is hot the girls swim in the *sloot* there, nearly naked). Boys from the workers' cottages nearby chucked stones at him and chased him off. In any case, last Thursday morning this Walker fellow was found hanging from a branch quite close to the bathing place. The police think it must have been an accident, that he probably climbed into the tree to escape from a dog chasing him, there's a vicious *boerboel* belonging to the farmer whose house was built where the river makes a shiny elbow, and that he tied himself to the branch so as not to fall off, perhaps he wanted to spend the night up in the tree, and that maybe he slipped and got strangled. The branches get slippery from the dew. But my friends all think it was suicide.

Don't you think Oumatjie Keet can rest in peace in her grave now? And you can stop worrying too? Even if it was neither accident nor suicide, but some people in the dark quietly helping him to realise his sexual fantasy of flying? Every dog gets its day, *ja-ja.*

BARRY

Early on a Sunday morning I go jogging with Revel. There's no traffic this early, the air is like a flower, fresh breath comes from the vineyards, we decide to run out of town on the Barrydale road. It winds along the valley floor, passing the municipal refuse dumps where people in tattered clothes 'farm' the rubbish, and then it climbs gradually. Before hitting Barrydale sixty kilometers further, it will rise and fall over the Tradouw Pass, an easy passage accessible even to women (*tra* means woman), and continue on to Ladismith, named after the wife of a long-ago governor, she was of Spanish origin, Lady Juanita Smith, and she bequeathed her Bible to the village.

The town of Barrydale evidently gets its name from the powerful Barry dynasty of traders and merchants, based in Swellendam but active all over these parts for most of the previous century. They ruled over a veritable empire, with its godowns and stores and banks; they even issued their own banknotes. They opened up the Breërivier for transport by water. Not many rivers were navigable in South Africa; one could go up this one as far as Malgas. Their steamer, the S.S. *Kadie* (Kadie was the name of a Hottentot *kraal* or settlement on the riverbank) became famous for its exploits. Its best-known voyage was when it took a load of coal to Simonstown for the *Alabama*, a Confederate buccaneer ship, wetting its hook there whilst preparing to pursue the Yankee *Vanderbilt*. On 17 November 1865, the *Kadie* with a powerful deathcry perished on the rocks at the mouth of the Breërivier. The *Cape Argus* wrote about her bones: "We have been so accustomed to see the plucky little craft with her red cutwater come in and out of the bay, that it is difficult to believe that she will not appear again." The loss of the *Kadie* signaled the beginning of the Barry empire's decline.

But I prefer to imagine that the town could as well be named after another, earlier Barry. His name was James and he too was a Scotsman. The life we have is mysterious. It is believed that he was brought up by two elderly bachelors who sent him to the toughest schools. After studying medicine, he joined the Colonial Army. Despite his slight build and pale countenance (and the gibes he was obliged to endure), he became an excellent rider and a skilled swordsman. In Cape Town he was the medical officer responsible for the well-being of His Majesty's prisoners; his virulent denunciation of prison conditions caused such a political uproar that he was forced to 'resign'. After a spell of administrative exile in Australia he returned to the Cape, where he was

appointed personal physician to the body of the governor, the affable ladies' man Lord Charles Somerset. Dr.
Barry showed extraordinary devotion and attachment
to his charge. He was plucky; also easily provoked.
First-rate shot, good hunter, held his drink with the
best, shy with women—he watched like a broody hen
over his master's honour. Time and again he had to fight
duels, particularly when rumours of the lord's amorous
exploits surfaced. (This was how he got to cross swords
with one of my ancestors, Sir Abraham Cloete.) When
Lord Charles Somerset retired in ill health to London,
the good Dr. Barry followed him. With Somerset's passing away, our man went to live in Edinburgh, where he
adopted a young black boy from the islands. At his
death his considerable savings, for he was a Scot all his
life, went to the boy, who promptly left Britain, presumably for the West Indies, slipping off the page and never
to be heard of again. And the old lady laying out Barry's
thin remains for decent burial to her stupefaction discovered (uncovered) the unused and shrivelled body of
a woman!

Revel chuckles when I remind him of this 'road to
Barrydale', he says I probably skewed a few facts, mixing befores and afters, but of course he is as intrigued
as I am by the life of this woman pretending all along—
why?—to be a man. But we don't laugh too much, we
need our breath for the run back. There's a Sunday silence in the air. Pale clouds will float high through the
day.

Around the last turn before re-entering town we
come across a lorry pulled off the road. Its windscreen
is shattered, splinters are strewn like diamonds over the
tar, two men—the white owner, a trucker from Barrydale, and his brown employee—stand cowering and

shivering close to the vehicle. This happened barely ten minutes ago, they recount, still shocked: they are on their way in an empty truck, a motorcar comes towards them from Montagu, not driving at high speed, there are no other vehicles on the road, a man leans out of the car and fires several shots, the intention must be to kill and the shooter must be well-practised because two bullets pass within centimeters of the driver's head, they never see the assailant or his weapon properly, the car continues on its way. (And we never heard a thing, perhaps because we were chortling and breathing hard.)

ELECTIONS

The elections usher in a confusing period. A thick-set young man called Servaas Botha knocks on the door of Paradys to try and convince me to vote for him, but what can he promise? (Instinctively I try and see whether he's inherited from his forefather Boetatjie the scar around the neck of a decapitated head.) Kwaaiman undertakes to be a candidate, he will stand as an independent in a brown ward. One day I accompany him when he goes canvassing for support. It is a depressing experience. Over the lower half of a kitchen door I see a woman in a house, one child on her hip and obviously many more around her knees, she gives a broad toothless smile. Out-of-work men in blue overalls complain about 'darkies' moving into the area, telling the brown people to bugger off, wanting to confiscate their houses—You have had your time under apartheid, it is our turn now. A broken-down taxi lies on its side in a ditch, the painted sign on the window says: "If all else fails, try lowering standards." A blind man is in his tiny garden with his dog, when the dog sees us strangers he starts howling, and the man yells—Quiet, you brute! Give us a minute of silence, you devil's hound! Have you ever heard *me* bark? A young man with greased hair is tinkering under the hood of his car, the seats inside (and the steering wheel too) are covered with thick artificial fur, on the side of the car is stencilled "So many woman, so little time." His friend laughs at my brother—he knows him. It turns out that he has been discharged from prison only recently. His neck and face are embroidered with tattoos, as if big flies have done their writing exercises on his skin and left other discharges as well. One line, neatly encircling the throat, reads: "You broke my wings, you bastards..."

Awful reports surface. In mortuaries police nick the money of the dead, particularly if they have been murdered or are casualties of road accidents, the notes must be rinsed to clean them of blood clots; they cruise certain city streets and pick up prostitutes, these are taken to the mortuary for carnal intercourse, afterwards they lock the ladies of the night in the cold chambers where corpses are kept; they kidnap a suspect and take him to the house of the dead for interrogation and force him to have sex with a cadaver... It is guaranteed to lubricate a man's tongue... Street children are enlisted by gangs, they move among the crowds, tap old people on the shoulder and immediately duck away unseen; false 'witch doctors' pitch up and ask the bewildered oldsters if they aren't perchance being molested by the invisible *tokkelosh* (Kaggen?), for a small price the witch doctor is willing to give some effective advice...

In Bath Street an old gent comes up to our car. He wears a jaunty feather on his sweat-stained hat, a faded college blazer, a bag of soft leather is strapped to his back, his face is yellowish and flat and his eyes a peculiar blue colour, he is very drunk. He explains that he has walked all the way from Springbok in Namakwland, he is a true member of the church and soon to be employed, and would you have some money for him? *Ek kan sien baas is nie 'n onbeskofte baas nie*, he says. (I can see you are not an uncouth master.) During the telling of his extended tale Lotus says *ja, ja*—without understanding a word. I give him money and immediately he starts negotiating for more . . . In Kogmanskloof, just beyond the Poort, I encounter an elderly nomad. He pulls along a handmade cart abundantly embellished with sign-boards, ribbons, tassels, pennants, flapping black sheets, drawings, strips of handwritten texts. The wind has many a tongue to pray with. He is clothed in a multi-coloured patchwork coat of his own design. His name is Outa Lappies (Old Father Rags). Life is a journey, he insists. It is a never-ending story. A man without the traces of his travels has no life to speak of. How can you remember if you have not travelled? He shows me his diaries—sketches of places and things over the face of the earth visited by him, the written worms of wis-dom which emerge from the night-house of his mind, still blackened by their trajectory. Where he stays? Why, wherever night lowers her cloak, provided there's a tree he can climb into. Trees are wonderful—they give you sticks for fire, you can chain your cart to the trunk, you can sleep safely among the branches. It is a venerable custom. Old Boere in this part of the world also used to hide in the trees . . .

One night I go with Kwaaiman to the rugby field, where a provincial politician will address a political rally. On one side the sky is being flooded by darkness, on the other the piercingly bright evening star is climbing above the sombre mountain-backs. The politician, a brown man, represents the National Party, our oppressors of yesterday. His thick-set wife sits on stage with him, she is the spitting image of a bourgeois white *tannie*—broad-brimmed hat, flowery dress over a corseted body, severely permed hair, powdered chin, perfumed hanky. She is handed a bouquet of flowers exactly the way her white predecessor would have been. The proceedings are opened by the prayer of a local minister, humbly inviting God to come down and help Thy servants, as if the house is not full of blood and shit! Some ANC militants in the audience heckle the speaker. He's a sellout, they shout. But the speaker is an old dog at this kind of game, he outwits them, he twists general laughter around his little finger, they stalk off in stiff dignity. The speaker (with his neat neo-Afrikaner political moustache) says: This is Afrikanerland, 70 percent of the people in the western Cape speak Afrikaans. It is only Afrikaans which makes of the Afrikaner an Afrikaner; without Afrikaans he'll look a lot like a Russian or a Jew. The language makes the mouth. He says: We need partnership across the colour line to save the country, otherwise we'll become like the rest of Africa. Don't believe the ANC with their sweet talk, the ANC is a loverboy who wants to undress you to steal your clothes, it is smearing fat around your eyes. He says: It serves no purpose to live in the desert and ask, oh dear God, please take away the sand so that I may enjoy myself. He says: The nurses in the hospitals (on strike) dance a *toi-toi* while the patients are dying, it is their victory celebration. He says (to the whites, sitting in the pavillion with lowered heads and repentant shoulders, hoping nobody will remember them from yesterday): Those here who have sinned and have seen the wrong of your ways, *you* must speak out, because you *know* about the fruits of evil. He says: Parliament, where even the security cameras have been unscrewed and stolen by new members, has become a flea market. He says (of the late Joe Slovo, in life secretary of the Communist Party and minister of housing) with a wicked lilt to his voice: Here lies poor old Joe with hands folded; never built a single house. (It rhymes in Afrikaans.) He says: They must keep their noses out of our affairs and their hands out of our pockets. While the food of the people disappears they have led your attention astray by saying: "Have you seen what nice shirts Mandela wears?" He says: What we need is a new Afrikaans name for the western Cape, a new flag, a new language monument . . .

On election day it rains. A flock of small brown kids are plashing naked in a hole turned into a pond of muddy water. Like sparrows they shake their wings. Kwaaiman is thrashed decisively. Outside the polling booth (a school) in Ashbury he argues with a pompous official who objects to Lotus picking *vygies* in the yard. What? When you people burn down schools and offices? Fuck off, man! . . . Two helplessly staggering voters are causing some disruption. One insists on doing his duty by *everybody*; his friend keeps demanding: Where'sh my money? . . . The old Englishman stops me in front of the post office. Years have closed his body like a rusty pocket knife, there are blue smudges around the eyes, the mouth with its long white lips trembles. With his hands like page-pressed butterflies he wishes to explain to me that with stiff resolve he remained at his post all along in support of his candidate, to fight for the good cause of all pets . . . I am reminded of something written by Herman Charles Bosman in *The Artist in South Africa*: "And Africa has much to teach us—of thought that is created in sand and ceremony and that life is an ancient ritual."

COMES THE PRESIDENT

Our president comes to town in a flashy shirt to bless the annual Muscadel Festival. (His handlers must be trying to divert his attention, or wear him out with tiring visits to insignificant places.) Can it be true, as somebody claims, that this is not the real Mandela? That he was 'turned around' in prison through brainwashing? Or maybe even killed and replaced by a look-alike?

We have guests: Buddy and his wife, Gerty. They have driven down from the interior in their big air-conditioned limousine to spend a few days with us. Buddy is very close to my heart. We drink much wine and we look at the mountains.

There's a welcoming reception for the president around the walled-in swimming pool of the local guest house. The foremost citizens are present—the pharmacist with the legs of a stork, the butcher with a moustache of two kilograms, the school principal and his patient belly, the mayor who has no past, the chairperson of the civics association with a lost future . . . (Kwaaiman has forbidden his wife, Miriam, to attend this fuss made of 'the chocolate prince'; she's in tears.) The president is escorted in, hard of hearing and stiff of step, as if he were some exotic animal on a leash. How are you? How are you? He smiles his leading-man smile to all and sundry. A white woman immediately imposes herself upon him (as if he were a servant) with a pile of books she wants signed. Now! He is given one of François Krige's drawings to remember his visit by.

The guest-house owner has applied repeatedly to join the local ANC but is turned down, presumably because of the minor matter of a white skin. The president shakes all the available hands, sees Buddy and me nursing our glasses in the back row, hugs me and says: Gee whizz, what are *you* doing here? (But this is home territory, Mr. President. Don't you know? Welcome!) He makes a speech to say how often during his long years in prison he'd heard about this beautiful town in the mountains with its sweet fruit. And so, today, etc.

People are allowed into his presence in one of the rooms, to whisper sweet nothings in the ear which doesn't hear. Then he moves off with his entourage and the security detail to go open the festivities.

We cross the street for a meal in Fred Schnozzel's eatery. Kwaaiman and Miriam have joined us. Her cheeks are still sad. Ingrid Weltz stands outside the restaurant to see the president, bent double, these people come to hawk and spit in our gardens, she carries a plastic bag, in the bag a big pistol is clearly visible, nobody seems to pay any attention. Carol, her helper, guides Ingrid to a seat inside. Carol's dog comes up to me, smiles like a politician, he has a strong smell, wags his tail, and starts mumbling a story with neither head nor tail, but Carol says not to take any notice, it is just gossip. The dog winks a worldly-wise eye.

The president's voice echoes through the village. Loudspeakers have been rigged up in the branches, birds are startled by the heavily accented Afrikaans. Bits and pieces surface. Down the street there's a barrier, you must have a ticket to proceed further. Kwaaiman is on duty at the gate, but he can't help it, he growls and then surreptitiously lets in for free the little barefoot brown boys with the big eyes.

A very old (and visibly affected) brown lady on the pavement embraces me. Isn't it wonderful that we should all be brothers and sisters now? What a lovely new South Africa! Yes, Buddy answers—and you should be proud that our president is here. What? the old lady screeches. That kaffir? They should explode a bomb in his face!

MEMORY

When he is small his mother chucks him and his brother away. (The father is fighting on a faraway front, the mother is a helpless drunk who dances alone at night.) Grandfather and grandmother take the two orphans under their roof. He loves his grandfather with boundless affection, a big man with red cheeks, a paunch and braces. When he is twelve years old his grandfather loses his way, one day he walks into the veld, towards the evening of the third day when the African red-nobbed coots are already quarreling with the shattered black mirror of the marshes, they find him under a thorn tree in the wind, hanged by his own braces. His buttocks are cold. Many years later he (my friend) gives me a glimpse of a dark heart of memories. In the meantime he does well—a leader in his field, respected, well-off, influential, everything under control. With the years his body puts on weight, starts resembling that of his grandfather so long ago. When he visits us in the small town on the edge of the dry interior, he is in good spirits. His motorcar shines, his cell phone chirps regularly, his wife has good teeth and her fingernails are painted red. In the morning he is gone and by afternoon he is not back yet. At dusk (there are gnats under the pergola) a shepherd tells of a strange man with a soft body, entirely naked, whom he saw wandering in the veld. The shepherd whistled but the stranger took no notice, and so he (the shepherd) sat on his haunches in the shade of a bush until he lost sight of the man, this way towards Duiwelskloof where mountains by day lie shivering in the white heat. A patrol goes into the veld with searchlight and loud-hailer and returns empty-handed. At first light everybody is called up—police and the local citizen force, workers from the canning factory, the bigger boys from school. Within shouting distance of one another we shall walk through the wilderness. Each one has a pocket mirror with my friend's name written in red lipstick. So that he may recognise himself. And not be confused by the image of his grandfather.

STONE

As for myself, as I disappear I have to think of something written by William Gass: "... remember me when I'm a ghost; watch me turn myself into a book."

Once upon a time, long long ago . . . Isn't this the way all stories start? Is a 'story' not an attempt to stop time at a moment of beginning and to take it from there in another direction? But it is true—long ago I wanted to return to this paradise to write about the light and the dust. To write myself one last time?

Earlier people didn't seem to have any curiosity about 'the deep past', they didn't go around exploring ruins. Or is it my imagination? Why not? Why have we become so obsessed with origins and beginnings? Surely it must be because of some alienation, because our so-called broadening of vision brought about a loss of recognition. Also, 'knowledge' before would appear to have been ritualistic—or maybe, I should say, it had to be re-enacted, repeated and echoed, to become 'understanding'. Nowadays it is supposedly 'factual', an assessment or a discovery.

And yet, the future is only an ever-extending present, like ripples spreading wider. We are already, and always, at the beginning of a new story, but we are not its origin. If we wanted to be theological we could say: God (or the act of creation) is the stone thrown into the dam. We are not sinking stone, but water, and the one 'consciousness' we have is that of movement, of rippling. Of course, a stupid question would be: Who threw the stone?

Now that we are arriving at the end of the trip, in other words, at the end of a given transformation, it is time to draw some conclusions. Nomadism is all about following the migrating animals of one's thoughts. Can they be impressions? Do they belong to me or do I belong to them?

Along the coast, especially higher up where vegetation is denser and greener and where the waves are full of hissing grey water, it often looks as if the sunset is applied in spray paint. Broad bands of clashing colours flare up, change, fade. But in the interior, and even more when mountains propose a place for going down into darkness, the evening is white. At times one experiences a barely noticeable bright shivering. It is the people who grow darker, not the land. First the people, then the house from the inside, then the garden. At last one thinks it is dark as far as one can see, one thinks that all light has been sucked from the earth, but it is eyewash.

Reader, I'm leaning forward to whisper to you, not to bother you or to ask you to hand me up a book, but to tell you that the ways of the mirror are dark to the eye. As you've noticed: not everything is 'true'! Writing is also in its own way a stone making the clear water of memory murky. Or maybe it is a Joseph Rodgers knife separating the head from the body. And because I have this tendency to abuse my friends and my family, to defame them even, to lie to them and about them, I thought it advisable to camouflage some names and to darken a few sources. One has to protect oneself. The rest is the verbal truth. All water and blood.

It is obviously one's manifest destiny to be double. This much I can see before returning to where I come from, to the outer darkness where there's a gnashing of wet teeth. One cannot unwrite what has been put down. The French poet Baudelaire—who appreciated the wine from Constantia, the estate which once belonged to my revolutionary forefather—says that one can only be an artist on condition of being double, and not ignoring any phenomenon of one's double nature. Fat excuse!

In the Montagu museum I found a reference to two brothers who must have been alive around the beginning of the century. They lived on adjacent farms near Almôrensfontein. They were very poor, those were desperately poor times, and the only money they had was one shilling. So one week Jan would go and work for Piet and at the end of the week he would be paid one shilling in wages. The next week Piet would be employed by Jan for a week's salary of one shilling. Isn't the founding principle of capitalism, and therefore of progress, that money should keep circulating?

I have in my possession a small, dark bit of family history. It is a tiny double portrait of our father, Hannes, and his brother, Oom Koot. It must have been made when they were in their early twenties and not yet married. Their hair is brushed back, cut short at the sides; they wear neckties, each with a tie-pin, and the collars are white and stiff and quite high. Behind the faces the two small photos would seem to be painted, probably a backcloth in some photographer's booth at a country fair. Both of them look solemnly straight into the camera's eye, and they have similar slightly lopsided smiles. Each photo is outlined by a heart shape. From the hearts two drawn hands extend to firmly grasp one another. And then there is written: "MIZPAH The Lord watch between me and thee when we are absent one from another." What does this photo celebrate? It must have been a standard postcard meant for lovers.

You, the dead child to whom I've been reporting (or that dog called Death?), have been with me like a shadow, the echo beyond the periphery of my explorations, since long even before I returned here to look for you. In Mexico I visited a museum some years ago and came face to face with a stone representation of Xolotl, the twin brother of Quetzalcoatl. In the Mexican tradition it is told that Xolotl stole a human bone in the

kingdom of the dead. He broke the bone, and from this act humanity sprang (maybe from the dark marrow). He holds his long tail in an open hand. I leave it to you to interpret the gesture.

MEMORY/MOTHER

You should know more about our mother. This could be a dream, but it is the image which lingers. My mother is dead. She is already lying in the coffin, dressed for eternity. She's talking, talking. (She was always full of words, our mother.) Her voice has a slight nasal quality. Sometimes she coughs from talking for too long without taking a breath. I want to make her sit up in the coffin and tap her between the shoulder blades to help her get her breath back. She's asking for lipstick, her lips are dry. I rummage among her things on the dresser, I have never seen my mother with lipstick, but I find a tube in a drawer, it must date from the time she was a young girl on the Nagwag farm. I redden her lips for her. A red kiss blooms on her pale face. Red is the colour of good fortune. Two men come into the room to put the lid on the coffin and screw it down. Then two more men enter to help carry the burden. My mother's voice is muffled. She mentions my name several times. There's a secret she wants to share with me. I remain behind. Her lips won't be dry. I hear the murmuring going down the corridor, growing fainter.

MEMORY/NAME

Many years ago, when I was already a married adult, I asked my parents why I have this name which sounds so much like an echo. After all, there must have been many other possibilities in the family: from my mother's side Hendrik or Schalk or Dawid (the uncle with the miraculous gift for taming birds) or Nico (the uncle who swung from the curtains); Stephanus or Koot or George (the black uncle) from my father's. No, my father said, this is the way it came about. Your Aunt Tina and Uncle Willy had a boy called Breyten. About ten years before you were born this Breyten, who must have been seven years old at the time, was sent by ship to Australia where Uncle Willy had family. The ship disappeared on the high seas, no wreckage was ever found. And so, when you were born, Aunt Tina pleaded with us to give you the name of her dead child.

Now, wherever I go, I find the trace. Kwaaiman says the family is closing in upon him. I meet a publisher with the surname Breytenbach and we try to figure out whether we're related. The publisher remarks with a snort that we'll never know. His father told him, he says, that a distinctive characteristic of the Breytenbachs is precisely that they move away from one another and then just don't want to know. When I tell this anecdote to Kwaaiman he fully agrees. He says: Luckily I (Kwaaiman) was given away to Aunt Tina when I was little!

BREYTEN DOG

Two weeks ago we drove in to Cape Town. Mercy, Adam's girlfriend, works for a radio station, she moves down the corridors on long legs, and she has arranged for Adam to interview me. We shall have a conversation about language and identity. During the interview I notice two thin white lines on Adam's wrists, like hairline cracks, but we don't speak about it.

When we emerge from the studio Mercy asks if she can introduce me to the sound technician. Why not? She is a young brown woman with earphones over her head, sitting in a booth behind a glass partition. She comes out to shake my hand, and tells me about a strange coincidence. Her father is a teacher and an activist. He followed my trial all those many years ago with great attention. And the day I was sentenced (she was only a small girl at the time) he went out to buy a puppy and he gave the pet my name, "So that somebody by that name can run around free outside!" Although the funny thing is, she remembers, she used to chase the dog around the garden, shouting: *Bedelaar! Bedelaar! Kom hier!* (Beggar, come here!)

The recording studios are situated in Sea Point. When the interview is over, we walk down to the sea. In the lee of the seawall separating the promenade from the beach a *lallapyp* (as we call them in prison, a 'pipe-sleeper', a homeless bum) and his very young woman have set up house. A few empty cartons, some rags. If they were to fall asleep while drunk, the incoming tide would certainly drown them right there. He is physically like a throwback to a previous age, a pure light-skinned Khoi with slanted eyes and high cheekbones. The earth is our womb. He must be from the interior where it is too hot for time to move fast—maybe from as far away as Springbok near the Gariep.

In the absolutely white sand they have scooped together a miniature Table Mountain, on the 'mountain' they have planted a paper South African flag and a little plastic bust of Jan Smuts (because of the goatee I'm

reminded for a moment of Oom Tao, the mountain philosopher), and right around this 'installation' they have
spelled out with shells and seaweed: WE WISH YOU ALL
A HAPPY NEW SOUTH AFRICA FREEDOM FOR ALL.

To me this heap of sand doesn't look like Table
Mountain at all, it is more likely a grave, and the miniature bust an appropriate headstone. (Here, symboli-
cally, lies White, and the gravedigger is a descendant of
the original inhabitants, the *Strandlopers* encountered on
this beach.)

While Adam talks to the poor beggar, cocking an ear
for a 'stifled voice' (who obviously wants money), I ask
Mercy about the scars I noticed on Adam's wrists. Is
that where the dog bit him? She turns her back to the
sea and looks up at the bulk of the mountain towering
over the city, clouds are like seagulls in the wind, her
lips tremble and her eyes are wet, she tells me softly
that no, no, it was really because he tried to cut the
veins in his arms, but I need not worry and I mustn't
tell anybody, please. And the dog too has been sworn
to silence.

THE SNAKE IN THE GARDEN

Lotus is shaping the grounds at Paradys plant by plant.
(The house has already been broken into three times
since we've been here, sacked and vandalised, there's
nothing much to steal, the small hoof-iron cemented
into the outside wall doesn't seem to impress the robbers, Kwaaiman says, *ja-ja*, what did you expect?)

A brown boy comes to offer his services for helping
out in the garden. I recognise him as the little chap who
got the fishhook into his own finger. His name is Eric

Fortuin and he's the grandson of the ancient gardener slowly and wide-eyed working for Sylvia Krige. His parents 'left' him (he looks away shyly when he has to talk around this pain), they are in Cape Town (maybe they sleep rough on a beach), and now he grows up with his grandparents.

The boy is willing, but not very effective. Lotus gives him as much food as he can eat, at night he can pick the fruit from the trees to take home. He claims to be older than his appearance suggests, though he's still only in primary school. The learning comes slowly. Says he knows his age for sure because he was born on 27 December, the day right after Christmas, *meneer*. Life cannot be easy at home. He has uncles who frequently drink *suurwater* (sour water, alcohol); then they fight. All he wants to do when he grows up is to earn enough money to buy a house for his entire family. (Already he must think: If only I can afford a house my parents will return!)

At night he has nightmares about a giant snake known to be guarding a water hole in the mountain. This snake (his grandfather tells him, and he should know, since he saw it with his own eyes, *meneer*) carries a big red diamond on its head. If only he could get hold of that diamond he would have enough money to buy a house big enough for his whole family! But it is a very clever and very huge and very dangerous snake, it can outrun any boy. The only way to fool it is to rub cow dung all over oneself so that he doesn't smell you coming. Maybe *meneer* will help him go and steal the snake's red stone?

Because how else is one to get a house? In the village there's a demonstration in favour of *masakhane*, the poor people are walking with poor banners in procession through the streets and they chant: *Sy's onse bruid, ons dra haar op die hande!* (She's our bride, we carry her on our hands.) But the money is not getting through; the authorities have only built a few matchboxes; the 'bride' is a virgin spinster.

Fortuin tells me about all the dangers lurking in the garden—the many shapes of snake, the *bloukopkain* (it must be a salamander), the spiders. There's an enormous, furry customer, very poisonous, he jumps a long distance and when he bites you (he says), you become paralysed, the 'hind parts' are as big as a man's hand. He refers to all black birds as falcons. The others he calls *kokkewiete* (boubous). In fact, the world is full of dangers. Even the doves chase him.

With the spade he kills a small snake. He comes to show me the mutilated remains, a word without sound draped over the blade. The devil's people won't leave us alone, he says. Isn't it so, *meneer?* It was Father Adam who got all mixed up with the snake. Yes, I suggest— but he sinned, he was looking for trouble. *Ag*, shame, the poor Adam, Eric Fortuin says.

IDENTITY/LANGUAGE

This is more or less what I tell Adam during our conversation in a soundproofed room: When one has had enough of prison and one wants to beat a retreat, in a figure of speech, it can be arranged that one is done away with. The procedure is really quite simple, it is even set out clearly in notices pasted to the walls of the barracks. You will report at the main gate that you intend to escape; there you are taken into custody and brought to the office of the superintendent. Exactly one

hour later (the guarantee stipulates) you will be exe-
cuted—strangled, hit behind the ear, shot or electro-
cuted, details can be negotiated—with the official
explanation, acceptable to all parties, that the mishap
occurred during an attempted escape ... When you are
new in that environment, when you are still an outsider,
you have to concentrate on learning the language properly. You must master it so that you can converse fluently when it is your turn to report at the main gate
(entrance and exit). In fact, the moment of decision is
entirely defined by your ability to use the tongue. You
surmise that this final hour in the superintendent's office, the *mano a mano*, the eyeball to eyeball in an enclosed space of forgetting, is the critical conclusion of a
transition. What will be said there? Is it the time of
explanations, confessions, concessions, justifications?
One wants to possess the language *inside* one, to be
ready and sufficiently unencumbered for the transcen-
dent act of stepping out.

After all, I should know that it is language which
makes me. I'm the Afrikaner, possessed with ideas, stubborn, unsure, parochial. Stupid but sly. Treacherous—
my morning prattle and my night tattle are cut from
the cloth which suits my interlocutor. Thus pliable,
adaptable. I wear shoes of soft grey leather, my wife has
a broad-brimmed hat and a flowered dress, her private
parts are powdered. I'm a racist, I think by rote in
groups and categories. My jokes issue from the nether
orifices of the body, and turn upon defecation. I'm the
Afrikaner, my granny was a slave woman. I live with
the sweet narcosis of words. My language speaks of the
loss of purity, I mix Europe and the East and Africa in
my veins, my cousin is a Malagasy; my tongue speaks
about moving away from the known, about overflowing

into the unknown, about *making*; of dispossessing, plundering, enslavement, mixing; of the transmission under guise of a 'new' language of that which refuses to be forgotten, of discovery but of agreement also (because comparison is as well a compromise), of the land and of light, of the art of surviving. I'm a Dutch bastard, my father is French and my mother is Khoi. Each grave in this purple earth is a place of exile.

I tell Adam that the only abstraction I'm still interested in struggling for is a community of understanding. Does it mean a sharedness? What is this ground of (I assume) mutual comprehension about? Language, obviously. Why language? Because it is the mother tongue (she was always full of words, our mother), because it is the dimension, the horizon, both the praxis and the product of consciousness. I may add that our specific language, Afrikaans, is the visible history and the ongoing process not only of bastardisation, but also of metamorphosis. (Bastardisation is a bleeding-in of images of different origins; metamorphosis is when the result is transformed into something totally different.)

Why could one not be as easy in a borrowed tongue, a second or third one which one learns later? Can it not be argued that there are other languages better adapted and more developed to express and transport the complexity and the diversity of the world we live in? And are there not other languages—Zulu, for instance— which are even more the products of rooting and fruiting in this native soil?

Yes, I answer, but language is not just a tool, it is perhaps the closest we can come to a communal 'soul'— because the sounds and the rhythms (all that which is not conveyed by epistemological 'meaning') flow, on the one hand, from a shared environment, and on the other from shared attitudes and knowledge conditioned by this environment. And because a language should not just be about communicating effectively, however sensitive a form of expression it may be, but also the contact with the inchoate, the pre-rational, the dark shadows flickering around the words: the 'deeper' sense of being. (Who is still interested in 'the deeper past'?)

Why? Well, I suppose because there is more to life than talking, and I'm less of a threat to others when I'm at ease with my own unelucidated origins. It has to do with belonging, see? It has to do with identity. Surely identity is at least partially affirmed by belonging, by being a member of a family or a clan or a tribe? And, surely also, knowledge rings true only when there's a share of throbbing under its surface?

I again wish to add that I find our language, Afrikaans, perfectly apt to pursue what I presume to be the specificity of a writer: "writing the self and rewriting the world." In other words, self-creation and revolution. (Ultimately a destruction of 'self'.)

I also wish to suggest that sharing the tongue, or the linguistic spaces (being at ease), is a pre-condition for mediating sensibly the other abstracts, such as freedom and justice and progress and so forth. Even of national unity in an area shared by diverse entities. (*I'm not sure I convince Adam there* . . .)

What is this 'shared environment' which needs the instinctive security of a mother tongue in order to be faced creatively? I'd imagine, physically: strangeness, harshness, unimaginable beauty, fire, sadness. And socially? Stupidity, cruelty, greed, violence, patience, generosity, hospitality, survival cunning, intolerance, strangeness, harshness, unimaginable beauty, fire, sadness. And formally? The rainbow nation. Soon African-ism. (Watch this space for the next hit!)

Is it only through language that you belong? No, I say; I may have abjured the identification of 'values', but there are other 'recognitions'; the land, the people, the history. But these are dangerous areas of accord, that much you're willing to concede? Sure! We are a mixture of different cultures which (or who), to start with, have opposing conceptions about land. The white part of our ancestry stole the land from the brown part of our ancestry. (Didn't 'progress' or 'development' make expropriation inevitable? And was there really a sense of 'owning' before?) For the settlers land was property to be cultivated and exploited as capital; for the herders it was nature, holy ground from where one came, to be used and accompanied but also to be left alone and feared and never to become static by ownership. And is it not so that the white writers, now that they live in cities, pine mystically for the land in order not to see the people?

The people? Tell me about the people. Can you share their prejudices? I don't know. I sometimes imagine that I know them well enough (I sometimes know that I imagine them well enough), and I have sympathy with them because I share the language of the territory and the memory, and therefore gleanings of the meaning. But there's an ambiguity here, a painful uncomfortableness. Partaking of the known can be a very effective way of camouflaging the unknown, or rather the unspeakable. It is like hiding in the light. Too much 'understanding' leads to complacency, and then corruption.

And the history? Do you take responsibility for the history written and silenced or effaced by our 'kind', slave owner and slave? Are your attitudes defined by the history of our ancestors? Are you the result and the depository of their memory? Take your stance to the English: You always get along well enough, and yet you don't like them. It is because of the Boer Liberation War? (As far as I know, no one closely related to you was involved in that one.) Is it because of their pretense of cultural superiority? Their capitalism and their liberalism? The fact that they're always on the right side, never responsible for any injustice, never have to question their assumptions? Is it because they look down on white and brown Afrikaners alike? (Not to mention the Indians and the blacks.) Is it because you don't like their nostrils? Is it because they have neither died enough nor killed enough to belong here? What a horrible criterion!

So this 'community of understanding' you're talking about is in reality a demarcation? The premise for exclusion and nationalism?

Yes and no. All I do know is that the dialectic between the 'own' and the larger togetherness, between the specific and the general—is creative and progressive and transformative. It is also never-ending, never resolved once and for all.

Because bastardisation, my dear Adam, cannot be turned back, believe me. But neither can one just escape from white into brown. One has to keep on making and finding oneself, and then *situate* and *orientate* that temporary find. You ask (in this soundproof room): What do you take with you of the old as you go over to the new? I can't help you. I know only that I find myself exposed on that edge of becoming. Consciousness in movement is not a calm sea. It is about perception and projection, it has to do with change—and the fear when one lets go, the illusion as well of becoming something 'better', the pain one experiences when one brings the roots to light. Perhaps you will think of it as running away from consistency, as escaping from responsibility. But try and see it as a journey of exploration into dark interiors (which, of course, have always been there). It is the discipline of drawing maps over the body of the other. And sometimes, often, mostly, it is the blind urge to survive. (But don't expect to be welcomed by the bourgeoisie!)

We should define more clearly the trajectory and the territory of the *métis*, the *baster*, the bastard, the hybrid, the creole—identify the 'colonies of reflection', the frontiers, the limits of integration. Are these lines of tension edges of creativity or barriers of exclusion? Our crucial contradiction of existence will remain: we are embarked upon a process of becoming other which is illuminated, step by step, by an awareness of differences (and of being 'different'). Within myself I too have to mediate the various components and strains which I embody, and around me I will have to compromise with groupings which may well be quite homogeneous.

Again, I can only say: There will be an awareness of *loss*, of leaving behind, of divesting yourself. (The more you get rid of the self, the more you become attached to yourself.) But it is good to travel to become poor. Explore the labyrinth of self as part of the history of creating consciousness, go through the underground, the sunken 'homelands' of imagination and memory where the rain bull dwells.

Which is why language is so important: as thread through the maze, as memory of change, as vector of imagination and intervention and invention. Our tongue is of the earth and of wind (which is death), of the concrete and the transcendental, of absence and ablution and exorcism, of the thing and the idea, of the uncertainty of absolutes and the absolute of uncertainty.

What do we lose? If we're lucky: monotheism, patriarchal or male-dominated 'values', the greed for power, the self-abasement of racism. (At least, the 'superiority' of the *white*.) What do we gain? Nothing much. An awareness of texture, which is an expansion of consciousness. And the deeper humanism which comes with the realisation that we are all movement and change. This is all I can leave you, brother. Not because I know better, but because we need to say these things to one another.

MEMORY

This memory which we have, to which we all contribute, which makes us, by which we are undone, this memory plays tricks on us. We cannot grasp it, we dare not look into its eyes because it will blind us with horror and shame. We notice it from the corner of our eye, it is making little signs at us from that zone between light and shadow, it flits through words and smells, it pretends to be wind, it surfaces from the land between deep sleep and waking. It taps one on the shoulder, one turns around, it is gone, today is blowing in one's face. I tell a story to my daughter, this is the way it is, and without my noticing, it twists my words out of shape. Before I know it, it is too late. I clasp my head to lament, and I feel the contours of a fish, very cold depth. I keep it imprisoned between pages, I open the book and find the droppings of a long-extinct bird, I breathe over it and the words are blown away like ash. I decide it doesn't exist, and it keeps on laughing inside me, like the aftertaste of an undigested meal. I pass it on to my dead

self, the dog infant, but he says: I've had it all along . . .
Memory is Kaggen, the trickster god. It says there is
one certainty: nothing is what it seems. It says there is
one finality: change.

GOING SOON

My mentor, Jan Rabie, is dying. I talk to him on the
telephone. He says the stories are now too deep to be
unearthed. He says the only thing now is to walk carefully, carrying the coals in an ostrich shell the way the
old people did, do be careful that the wind doesn't ex-
tinguish your memory of fire, and just pretend the
smoke doesn't make your eyes smart. He says that, as
for himself, he will sort of fiddle about, talk to the wood
that needs to be spliced for next winter.

My friend, Daantjie Saayman, is dying. (He will die
and lie very still, the trick is just not to breathe, and
when nobody is looking he will sneak away and walk
into the mountains.) A brown poet comes to visit him
to wish him a safe journey, he brings along his son who
plays the guitar, together they sing the poems of changing worlds.

My brother Bruinman has a big argument with the
people close to him who hope he can calm down, now
that the war is over. No, he shouts. He wants to go back
to war. He doesn't want to die fat and deaf like dough
in a chair. He wants to fight for Afrikaans. He leaves
his car in the middle of town where he is supposed to
live in retirement and stalks off. Even the priest can
give no advice to the imploring family. The priest prays
but God's eardrums were impaired by the last war. They
find my brother the next day, far away in the bush, he's

walking 'home'; no, he doesn't need transport, he can find his way by the stars and the smell of the wind, he's a soldier.

TRAVEL MEMOIR

One last swing through Heartland, and then time to go. I think of that flight out, cramped and noisy, sitting with knees drawn up below the chin, as entering darkness— the last stage into death.

We shall spend a few days with Freek and Iza at Kleinbos. This is the outside limit of our territory. On the way we stop at the Van Loveren wine estate to buy the necessary. The materfamilias, Jeanne Retief, has been keeping to her bed for quite a while now. Something is wrong with her leg, she cannot walk, a doctor operates on the knee but the swelling doesn't go down, she's in pain. We are taken through the copse of planted trees (all the famous names moving in the wind) and the rose garden, into the house to see her.

The house has been darkened to keep it cool. One light is trained on a painting on the wall—a rather garish depiction of sunset over the enflamed Montagu mountains. Jeanne Retief's face is smaller than we remember it, her eyes are drawn to slits. But her talk has lost nothing of its vivacity. What do we think of the painting? We smile and mumble and cough into our hands and smile again.

It was painted by Maître Pierre de Moncul, the local artist who swishes around with cape, carved walking stick and small 'intellectual' glasses. (In fact he's a charlatan called Piet Poephol.) The painter had an exhibition, he called Jeanne to tell her he made a work especially with her in mind, her son must drive her to Montagu, he grumbled and she was in pain, at Maître Pierre's house the painting was on show in the garden, Maître Pierre and his wife made Jeanne comfortable in the shade facing the painting (his wife was dressed in a cape, sandals, broad-brimmed hat—they're so *artistic*, Jeanne sighs), they brought her tea, they withdrew on tiptoe "to let her soul breathe," they put on a disc of Chopin music and opened the windows wide so that the soothing sounds might flow out into the garden, the birds tilted their heads. How could she resist?

Tea is brought into the bedroom by an elderly brown lady. Discreet clink of cups against saucers. Home-baked rusks. Jeanne points out the watermark on the wallpaper showing how high the Great Flood reached, a good hundred and fifty centimeters. She sighs. A friend of hers, an old woman living alone on a neighbouring farm, was butchered to death last night, in her own bed, the sheets all dirtied. For no apparent reason. Nothing was stolen. Maybe just the thrill of dislocating a life, of dipping hands in warm blood.

On to Swellendam. Usually we just drive through. When I was small Oom Frikkie and Ta' Johênna van Eeden lived on a farm in the district, they cultivated medlars and quinces, the trees were always agitated by a grey wind. Ta' Johênna must be a half-sister to my father. The old couple were raising an adopted boy with a shaven head, his name is Vrede (Peace). Kwaaiman claims that our parents gave him, Kwaaiman, away to Ta' Johênna when he was only a baby. He will always show the unhealed wounds of the foundling.

The Drostdy, residence of the *Landdrost* (highest administrative official), was the outpost of Company authority over reluctant and rebellious *burgers* (citizens) living beyond the mountains. It is both a gentlemanly mansion and a farm dwelling in Africa. Some rooms have floors of peach stones, in others the broad yellow-wood floorboards creak under one's tread, the long corridors are paved with shale slabs.

Along the walls of these passages old maps are exhibited. Explorers advance into the interior, try to colonise the untamed and the unknown by the giving of names. The maps of knowledge are partly the residue of observation, partly the wide arc of their imagination groping towards where experience and desire abut on the borders of the unknown, which will be sensed as 'darkness'. Life stories become drawings on paper. One map, in French, identifies the areas occupied by different Khoi tribes. It is clear that each of these 'nations' has its own 'country', right up to the Cape. A later map outlines the spread of colonists' farms, each with the name of the master—a new patchwork covering the older meaning of indigenous cattle farmers. A third gives us all the names along the seaboard, the outer rim, the smoking line of demarcation from where penetration can proceed—capes, coves, creeks, bays—mostly in Portuguese or French, often evocative. Most of these names will be covered by sand, the vowels of larger histories and broader horizons to be replaced by local Anglicisation.

In the *voorhuis* (front room, parlour) two small paintings catch my eye. Clumsily drawn, in any event already without the elegant dexterity of Europe. Representations of a man and a woman in a neutral space which is neither inside nor outside. Both are seen in profile, seated on chairs in the immensity of this continent where the sun shouts with a deafening yellow sound. One Jan Hendrik Crous, 21 November 1822, at Swellendam, and Johanna Dorithea Geldenhuis, 'portraited' 14 July 1823, both by J. P. Keet. I rejoice at the thought that this may be a forefather on our mother's side, an itinerant painter trying to pin down the transgression of borders.

Slightly down the hill lies Mayville House, restored to its earlier glory of a blend of Victorian and Cape Dutch architecture and furniture. We visit parlour and dining room and kitchen and pantry. Then the bedrooms with their high beds and their washbasins sunk in stands and tables. In the girls' room I see with a shudder of recognition a framed scroll with decorative letters: "My Grace is sufficient for thee." Did my mother, as a young girl, see this picture on the wall? And did it stay with her, this idealised and carefree space of taste, with sunlight filtering in through tiny window-panes? Do we at the end remember ourselves the way we were when the world was young, full of music and picture albums and scented love letters? On her grave-stone of dark granite planted on a slope outside Hermanus is carved: *My genade is vir julle genoeg*, the same words as on the framed scroll.

(I take along two images from Swellendam, both about two hundred years old. In one, rebel farmers and citizens from a short-lived Swellendam Republic march to Cape Town to help repel the invading British; they do so under revolutionary flags and slogans. The rumour of liberating ideas in Europe has reached this outpost. It doesn't do much good, their heart is not in the battle, the regular forces are routed, they get drunk: the Colony is lost to the British and the last Dutch officer to command the castle, a colonel incongruously called Gordon, shoots himself through the head with his pistol ... My second image: The old grandmother of a very highly esteemed family dies, her body is washed for eternity, at last a corpse attendant removes the wig without which the old white missus has never been seen, and discovers the crinkly hair of a half-caste.)

At Kleinbos wine and *snoek* (barracouta) await us, and the ocean's thunder ever in the background. The new-moon storm which brought lashes of rain to the interior must have been quite violent beyond the horizon. The beach, deserted as ever, shows the vomit—bottles, drift-wood, demijohns, plastic bags, remains of baskets and crates, lengths of rope—all probably thrown overboard by passing vessels. Even a hat filled with water.

During winter Freek registers as many as 21 whales in the bay. They come here regularly to calve. (It is an exceptional year—up to 360 southern right whales are counted along the coast from Muizenberg to Pletten-berg Bay, of which 109 will be new calves; also schools of dolphins, smooth shimmering seamstresses gracefully stitching surge to breakers.) He says you can watch the cows teaching the young about surviving in the deep. They swim out with their offspring, a little further every day, until they do not return.

Maybe it is because of the rough wash that a dwarf whale is beached. Or could it be the presence of larger predators deeper in? Do whales, like elephants also, die in enigmatic ways to tell us something about the planet? Freek and a friend go into the water to try and prevent the bulky mammal from committing suicide. They keep on turning the animal's nose towards the deep. Repeat-edly they swim with it to behind the foam line of break-ing waves, and each time the animal insists on coming back, looking for its death. It is late afternoon before the two exhausted swimmers succeed in guiding their charge back to the sea's safety.

Today I won't be able to run on the sand. A multitude of bluebottles washed up and are left in defence lines by the withdrawing tide. The water is still angry, wind whips foam off the waves and blows the suds to way beyond the high-water mark. Deeper among the dunes I come across the tracks of small buck. In the dense scrub of coastal *fynbos* I chase up a rabbit, and one may encounter puff adders, lazy like unavowable dreams. Once I saw a jackal trotting in the distance, lopsided because of the wind, leaving prints like delicate sand shells.

A pile of shells indicates that *Strandlopers* lived here centuries ago. One may still find sharpened stone tools, probably used as knives and arrowheads. A theory suggests that these people eventually became impotent because of the high concentration of iodine in their seafood.

Light is blinding, the merciless language of a sword. From here southwards there is no more world, one can see the curve of the earth, and on the far side (always the far side) there is endless darkness, finally the white stillnesses of Antarctica. A ship on the skyline is a crumb to a blue mouth, soon to be swallowed by distance.

We drive along the sandy track towards Vleesbaai (where passing navigators negotiated for meat), then Visbaai and Fransmanshoek (Frenchman's Corner, where a French schooner was impaled upon the rocks). Further along there will be Cape Vacca and Bull Point. Some of the old names, at least, are still alive. Anglers have thrown their baited lines to beyond the boomers, an onrush of water surges in white arches and trees and fountains against the rocks. The men watch us with dead eyes. They have emptied enormous bottles of alcohol.

A few days ago a yacht perished a little further east. The boat was tipped over by a freak wave and one crew member immediately disappeared in his watery grave, his two companions desperately clung to the upturned keel, the strong current took them fifty kilometers along the coast before they washed up on the rocks. A farmer, high on his dune, early the next morning noticed the two bloodied bodies on the beach.

The Western Cape Synod of the Dutch Reformed Church appoints a commission of enquiry to study the historicity of the prophet Jonah's claim that he spent three days in the whale's belly before being spewed out on exile soil. It is a painful quarrel—coming from a gathering of clergymen who never, during all the dark years of anguish, found any biblical grounds for contesting the church-sanctified oppression based on skin colour. Either you believe what Jesus said (that he'll rise from the dead after three days the way Jonah spent three days in the stomach of the fish), or you say Jesus was a liar—one heavyhearted brother complains. And the synod also decides that the Bible's authority must be accepted fully and should not be interpreted in any way that would water down this authority.

Dune farms run down to the sea, providing grazing to the thin beasts of impoverished owners. For generations the poor farmers here have 'farmed backwards'. There's intermarriage, and many 'take wife' illegally. 'Degenerates,' people say. Some are considered weak-minded, or it is thought that they've long since forgotten the little civilisation they once had.

Some of them keep ostriches, and we see the birds pacing up and down along the fences. They look exactly like retired Bolshoï ballet dancers: long sinewy necks, small heads with heavily made-up eyes and false eyelashes and the hair pulled into tight buns behind the ears, long legs with knobby knees, splayed feet which have seen better days, the toes all rough and callused and wide from too much dancing.

Descendants of the original beach dwellers are returning to the area. Smoke curling from the low vegetation stretching to the sea indicates a squatter camp. Jobless people without past or future. Intruders? The new dispensation says they may not be prosecuted. Will somebody look after them? No, nobody. What are they to live on? A little theft and some minor murders, maybe other illegalities compelled by necessity.

Then Bredasdorp. To look for some evidence of my mother's extended family. Quiet, sleepy place. The hill overlooking the town is appropriately called Soetmuisberg (Sweet Mouse Mountain).

The 'book of local history', in this instance, is called the Shipwreck Museum. We admire the hefty helm of the S.S. *Kadie*. There are records of a Portuguese East Indiaman which came to grief on the reefs off Cape Agulhas (Cape of Needles, the continent's southernmost tip), 16 April 1686. On board there were a Siamese delegation on their way to the court of Louis XIV. Silk and incense were lost. The survivors walked all the way to Cape Town; suffering from hunger and thirst the "mandarins were compelled to eat their shoes." Only a small group reached the Dutch fort twenty-four days later.

On 15 May 1871, a dark and blustery night, a Frenchman, *Le Souvenance*, was wrecked off Quoin Point. The ship carried 14 'white' crew members and 371 Chinese, the latter emigrants on their way to Jamaica. The French consul in Cape Town delegated a local farmer, Mr. Hugo (he must be a Huguenot with some French left), to write a report. "Amongst the wreckage we found the body of a man, which, like a wild animal, was covered from its feet to its head in hair, no longer than that of a cow." (The French text says *"cadavre noir."* A fortnight later Hugo wrote to the consul once again to suggest that it may have been an orangutan.)

Bad year, this 1871. The *Queen of the Thames,* on her way to the Cape from Australia, was lost with all hands off Struis Bay, her belly ripped open by submerged rocks. There was only one survivor, but he was a stowaway, so he decided to stay on board; looters found him two days later among bales of wool bobbing in the ship's saloon, playing the piano. (Many farmhouses in the dunes have as heirlooms coins and crockery and beautifully carved chests: booty, 'gifts from the sea'.)

The figureheads of these vessels always seem to wash ashore intact. We stand in awe before the voluptuous lady who once protected, tits in the wind, *Nostra Signora de los Milagros,* and the stern but proud figure who lorded it over the prows of *Willem de Swijger . . .*

In the burial ground all the graves face north, their backs to the town and, some ten kilometers away, the sea. A pity—the view on the town with its white walls, its red and green roofs, is quite pretty.

We find the double resting place of my maternal grandparents. "In loving memory of Racel (*a spelling mistake*) S. Cloete née Keet 25.1.1873–18.9.1942, and Johannes H. Cloete 7.2.1871–17.3.1958."

A section of this garden of peace is reserved for the small graves of angels, now hardly more than effaced memories of caved-in thoughts behind a low wall or a few bent spikes of wrought iron. Only the names are marked: Lottie, Kobus, Mattie, Annatjie Goldie, Jurie (Jackie), Benjamin, Trudie, Beatie, Margaret ("She's not

dead, but asleep"), Fransie, Joy, Pietie, Amor, Mavis, El-
mina, Baba Uys, "A small son of Herman and Maria,"
a nameless Cloete, Kleinding (Little One) van Zyl,
Banus ... Quite close by, a mysterious Hendrik Cloete
Goldie, 1868–1931, lies buried quietly.

BONNIEVALE/GOODBYE

Bonnievale. To say goodbye. Drive in along the irrigation ditch which my father helped build. Shiny sheet of
Breërivier to the right. One hundred 'boys' plus foremen
and overseers blast a tunnel through the hardest rock
in Africa. A twelve-hour shift with three men on the
drill advances six feet; they are paid two shillings per
foot. Rigg, the owner of all the land and the initiator of
the project, says: I hope to come this way in a boat
within six months. Now six million gallons of water a
day flow through the cement canal. When it is hot,
brown children bathe in the *sloot.*

C. Forrest Rigg buys 18,200 acres for ten thousand
pounds. It includes the original Bosjemans Drift con-
cession, which had been leased to a Van Zyl by the government. This is round about 1906. The best barley and
potatoes of the region are grown here. (After the crash
in the price of ostrich feathers Oupa Jan plants potatoes.) Farmers pay fifty pounds per acre for Rigg's land,
they can settle their debt over a period of ten years,
may acquire between two and twenty-four acres per
family, will have full water rights. Most of those who
buy come from the Oudtshoorn district. With irrigation
they can grow lucerne. With lucerne they can farm with
ostriches.

All is vanity. Rigg's darling daughter, Myrtle, blond,

blue-eyed, dies in 1912 at the age of seven. He and his wife Lilian have a stone chapel built for Myrtle just outside town, close to the cemetery where Oupa Jan and Ouma Annie lie. There are shadows in broad daylight. The intricately carved chapel door is imported from Zanzibar, the floor tiles from Italy. Inside there's a faint portrait of the little girl, her face nearly completely eaten away by mildew.

We have lunch at the hotel with cousin Aletta. She explains the family to us. Ouma Annie Olivier had three children from her first marriage: Aunt Miemie Wolhuter, Aunt Johênna van Eeden, Uncle Michal Olivier. Oupa Jan also had three from his first wife, the one who died from the snake: Aunt Tina Campbell, Uncle Jors (George, the black one), Uncle John. And then they have three together: Koot, Hannes, Nick. Aletta says old Mr. Rigg died at sea, was slipped under the waves. His wife, Lilian (a girl Moon), lived for many years more in a stubborn house on the hill overlooking the cemetery and the grey chapel with the stained-glass windows. At Christmastime, every year, Mrs. Rigg offered a cooked goose as a present to our family. Aletta had to fetch it. She went up the hill and waited in the kitchen, but she was very scared: old Mrs. Rigg had a tame white parrot walking around unfettered. This parrot loved to blow up its feathers and would curse shrilly to scare children. So Aletta came tumbling down the hill.

The official records show that *oubaas* Rigg had only three children. The first two died relatively young; Myrtle, the angel, at seven. They're all buried in the small churchyard around the chapel, and so are the Moons, the family-in-law. But in the memorial chapel there's a framed yellow news clipping, given by Rigg's grandson. Where does he fit in?

A few years ago a lanky Englishman, advanced in years, arrived in town. It was a Sunday afternoon. His name was Walker, he said. And he was Rigg's descendant. He had papers and certificates to prove it...

Rigg was married a first time, to a girl called Petronella. With her he had two boys. One went down in history without a gurgle or a wave. The other son emigrated to Australia. After Rigg's death, his second wife, Lilian Moon, kept up a correspondence with the family in Australia. Once, when a Captain Campbell from Robertson visited Australia, they even sent a white parrot to Lilian as a token of their respectful attachment.

Mr. Walker is a grandson. In his old age he comes across this correspondence and the newspaper cuttings telling of the irrigation scheme. Does the project still exist? And the stone chapel? He has to know.

I pretend I must go and buy a newspaper in the Oasis Café. Aletta thinks I was born in a house attached to this little store, which displays trinkets, cheap potatoes, comic books, various pies and cakes. They sell something called 'Russians'. Russians?

It is not the kind of place where one lingers. A nondescript middle-aged woman with an apron behind the counter. Flies around the mouths of the glass jars in which sweets are kept. A few faded advertisements. Three brown labourers have come in to buy cool drinks while I leaf through the newspaper. I ask them about the violence all over the country. Are they afraid? They laugh with wide wet mouths showing gaps where their front teeth used to be. One shakes his head and says: We talk every day to the Lord and tell Him this must stop now. Two laughs and shakes his head and says: When I walk out of my house I call His Name. Three shakes his head, laughs and says: We just eat forward; one eats of this, and then of that too.

A band of small boys come into the café, pushing and giggling. One of the workers shouts: Can we have a minute of silence here, you sons of the Devil? We all laugh. One can tell by his attitude that he is joking. Two says: Look high, look low! Three says: *Ja-nee*, this has always been a violent country.

EPILOGUE

Something remains to be told. A few days ago, before visiting Kleinbos, Lotus and I went to the museum once more. The old brown woman selling concoctions there (she remembered us fondly), showed us Mrs. Keet's medicine bag. We opened it and found two tiny crocheted bonnets inside, a white one and a black one. If the baby lived after birth, it was given a white one; if it was born dead, or died, it got a black one. There was nothing else in the satchel.

Then we went to the cemetery. Plovers with flat heads and long stemlike red legs were everywhere, it seems to be their favourite breeding ground, they jeered and taunted, then flew up and circled us with awful shrieks.

We didn't find Oumatjie's grave anywhere. (Under a cypress tree there's a scattered gravestone of a person called Keet—it could be that of her husband, but in that case he was much older than she was; somebody has fitted the pieces together like parts of a jigsaw puzzle or like the shards of a mirror.)

But then, there are anonymous heaps of soil every-

where, sometimes with a faceless, toppled-over headstone, at other times just a big stone to mark the place,
more often nothing. Nothing to show. Remember me?

We appropriate one of these unclaimed graves and
try to make it neat. Lotus finds an empty jam bottle
and I go look for flowers—purple jacarandas, red bougainvillea. This, we decide, will be the last resting place
of Rachel Susanna Keet.

We'll take this one, the one lying in the open with a
view all around on the immensity of mountains.

The "coloured" town is right next to the cemetery.
They won't give us away. Nobody needs to know.

I'm planting a beacon in Africa. A landmark. Am I
not allowed to mark out my history? May one not adopt
a dead person? It will not harm anybody. Don't worry,
there's nothing I want. Underneath the soil surely only
soil is left.

DUSK POEM

dusk brings flames to the evening sky
and our shadows grow long
as with the early hours,
we turn our backs on the Cape of Needles
where this continent slips into the ocean,
the coast is littered with shipwrecks like the empty armour
and caparisons of dragons,
from the mouth words wash over the page,
and ride over the Rûens where hills
are slow and good and silvery white with stubble,
a fire's crackling flags up above
and all about us the glow of dying
where silvery white sheep still nibble on the day's
stubble, for death is ripe,

the enchanting landscape of time
and longbreath movements of a memory
of so many skylines and conclusions laid away,
so many foregoers are dust underneath evening's
earth, two blue cranes rise flapping
and away on heavy wings,
to Stormsvlei, over Riviersonderend
through the gorges to Mooivallei:
at Wakkerstroom ultimate sparks
enkindle the coals to stars,
aloes are sentinels in the dark hours:
when night is a shed of old old moments
you may expect us at Paradys